The Brothel Bible

"THE CATHOUSE EXPERIENCE"

The Brothel Bible

"The Cathouse Experience"

BY

Sisters of the Heart

BROTHEL BOOKS

Sisters of the Heart Publications

Sisters of the Heart Publications
P.O. Box 94534
Las Vegas, NV 89193

Printed in the United States of America

First Printing: September, 1997
Revised Edition

ISBN: 0-9657525-1-8

LCC: 97-66353

Cover Photo by Ryan Pennell

This Book
is dedicated
to
All of our Sisters,
those working and those retired
We love you.

ACKNOWLEDGEMENTS

I thank the countless men who have shared themselves with me, for through them I have learned that sex is not love. I thank my husband for loving me, for sticking by me, and allowing me to make discoveries for myself. I thank the girls who have contributed stories and have edited this manuscript. Thank you Ryan, Russell, Sheri, Harry, Lynn and Frank for all the hundreds of hours of emotional support and encouragement.. I thank God for guiding me when I did not know which way to turn.

AUTHOR'S NOTES

I was 44 when I went to work in the Nevada Brothels as a legal Prostitute. It was my way of coping with "Middle Age Crisis". I'm sure I was also trying to seduce a 24 year male companion I was seeing at the time, into believing I was still young and attractive. Of course he was gay, but I thought I could change all that.

In hindsight, I'm sure a strong dose of sexual addiction and looking for love in all the wrong places and approval through sex also played a large part in my adventure. But at the time, I was oblivious to those deep-seated emotional traumas and realms of inner turmoil. I was just having fun playing "dress-up" -- after all, where else could I go all "dolled-up" in long sparkly evening gowns seductively cut (ala Mae West) with gobs of glittery jewelry and long blond wigs (ala Dolly Parton). And I don't think K-Mart patrons would have approved of me parading up and down their aisles in my thigh high red patent leather boots with 6" spike heels, wearing a skimpy red vinyl one piece costume with my pushed-up double-padded bra, long red velvet gloves, red flowers in my hair and blood red painted lips.

I got a complete face lift during my second year of working and wore gobs of rhinestone jewelry and wigs to detract from my aging physique. I would stand in "line-ups" in the brothels before potential customers trying to get picked with girls half my age on both sides of me . Fat chance I'd think, as I stood next to the clean, fresh faced, girl-next-door types, young innocent looking 20 year olds who were my competition and could be my daughters!

But, I glittered, as if I were a Show Girl (or so I tried to portray the illusion) and guys ate it up. After driving from Reno or Vegas out to the Ranches (which were always out in the middle of nowhere), yet allowed to legally exist, but carefully hidden far away from the decent folks in the cities and their puritanical prying eyes, guys (into their own emotional fantasies, spells and illusions) would surprisingly pick me. I figured they were fantasizing about getting it on with a Show Girl -- their interpretation of a Show Girl anyway -- probably the kind they'd just seen in the Topless bars in town combined with my brazen interpretation.

I worked about six months each year until I was 48. I'd stay in the Brothels for one to three weeks at a time -- literally locked up inside -- supposedly for medical protection. Many houses actually had the windows boarded up and sealed shut, without even a glimmer of daylight shining through. But management needed to control the illegal drug usage or authorities would shut the houses down, or so they said.

We were a motley crew of girls, ranging in age from 21 to 50 -- all sizes, shapes, types and colors living together kind of like a big slumber party or reminiscent of a college dorm. Some girls were there to support children, others to earn money to go to school, others needed cash to support their pimps (or financial advisors as the 90's terminology has it) or drug habits, or some just wanted extra spending money.

The customers would come from around the world, 24 hours a day, non-stop. We would get up and down all night long, taking cat naps whenever we could. There were lonely men (newly divorced or widowed), curious men, horny men, sexually addicted men, young bucks looking for excitement, older men wanting to feel young again (very often picking the youngest looking women). For whatever reasons they kept coming, escaping their realities, fantasizing for a brief moment, wanting to experience and be part of an illusion, captured in a state of euphoric bliss.

We'd leave after our tour of duty with wads of cash, bills stacked high. We'd make anywhere from $2,000 to $10,000 a week, depending on who you were, what Ranch you were working at, what season it was, and how many customers you'd serviced. But we'd spend it fast as we'd get it to keep the pimps happy, to keep up our physical illusionary sexual allure, or to buy drugs or alcohol, or for physical survival needs and family necessities.

The routine started getting old after a couple of years. It was turning into just plain old fashioned hard work. The glitz started to wear off, but the money was so good, I got stuck. Then I decided that I'd rather write about this business than keep doing it. So I organized some dairies I'd been keeping since I started in this profession and got a couple other girls to add their stories. I worked diligently on my computer (which I kept in the closet in my room in the Brothel) and I'd write in between customers - simply closing my closet door when I did "line-ups".

"THE BROTHEL BIBLE" is the first book of a series. This is a general introduction to the mysterious World of Brotheldom - - that World that sparks so many people's curiosity buttons -- men and women alike would keep whispering to me "What really happens there?" "What's it really like?" So, we've tried to be straight forward and answer those questions - "Who, What , When, Where, and Why?" We've tried to answer those questions you've always had, but never really knew who to ask -- to peel back the mysterious veil shrouding the legal Brothel Industry in Nevada -- the last frontier of legal prostitution left in the United States.

We've tried to cut through the stigma that has labeled working girls as "bad people" that have nowhere else to go or nothing better to do with their lives. We hope you will find that these girls are people, just like you and me, with the same emotions, problems, needs, wants, desires, brought to their jobs by circumstance and choice, to fulfill emotional needs as well as financial survival needs and wants and desires, coping with the changes in their lives -- lured to the glitz of Nevada just like you and me, by the glow of lots of quick money, enveloped in the fantasies that money and glamour can bring, as well as being caught up in addictions and unfinished emotional trau-mas from our past.

I feel like I've been doing research for four years now, by experiencing first hand the life of a legal Nevada Prostitute in a hands-on environment, and I am sharing those facts I've dis-covered with you in "THE BROTHEL BIBLE". I've been retired for a year now with no intent of ever returning. I just got married, am in extensive therapy for my addictions and trying to integrate myself back into the world outside of Brotheldom. I got pretty emotionally distant by being locked up for weeks at a time, isolated from family and friends, whisked away into a fantasy world.

Sisters of the Heart

"A Sister of the Heart"
Spring 1997

"Each of us have our own brothels to overcome, our own bondage to sex, love, fantasy, intrigue, and addictions."

CONTENTS

CHAPTER FOUR

CHAPTER FIVE

CHAPTER SIX

CHAPTER SEVEN

CHAPTER EIGHT

PROLOGUE

BROTHEL GLOSSARY

PREFIX

The Brothel Bible has been compiled by Sisters of the Heart, former working girls, who have experienced life in the legal Brothel Industry of Nevada. We have chosen to compile this information for those men and women out there who are simply curious, for those that have never frequented a legal Brothel, and for those customers who want to experience the true inner sanctums of our private world. Our source of information has come from our own personal experiences, research and diaries. We have written this book to break down that unspoken "Mystique" that seems to surround the Brothel Industry.

We have seen, heard, watched, listened, observed and absorbed experiences throughout these years by working alongside girls from all walks of life, and servicing customers from around the world. We have worked in a variety of environments, north and south, from plush houses with tiffany chandeliers, to run down double-wide trailers. Sometimes we've even found ourselves imprisoned in Brothels with locked gates, boarded windows and armed guards. Sometimes, we've lived like a Princess and sometimes like a Pauper. We've been higher than a kite, earning hundreds of thousands of dollars a year

*"A Sister reading and editing
The Brothel Bible"*

to being desperate, lonely and broke, living from motel to motel, or out of our cars.

As we write these words today, the feelings and memories of our experiences are alive within us. They range from satisfaction and excitement to resentment and rage. It is our desire to share these diverse emotions with you. This is not a clinical examination or objective review of Brothels. This is "The Cathouse Experience" and our goal of communicating it would fall short of it's mark if we were to sterilize and objectify what we have written.

We hope you enjoy the old time illustrations we found which we have used throughout this book. We thought they were fun. Since as authors we are remaining anonymous, so will our acknowledgements. But those of you who have contributed know who you are and our heart embraces each and every one of you -- for we are all "Sisters of the Heart".

The Brothel Bible

"THE CATHOUSE EXPERIENCE"

CHAPTER ONE

The Road To Brotheldom

Well John, you finally figured out a way to get to Nevada. You have a great excuse, your company is attending a convention in Reno or Las Vegas, or maybe a few of your friends or business associates want to get together for a little R & R. Yes! This is the "Adult Playground of the World", and what better place to play a little golf, gamble, see some great shows and be royally pampered and entertained.

You get here under the guise of a little R & R or business, but you really have a hidden agenda -- you long to visit a Brothel for once in your life. You've been hearing all these rumors and stories from other men that have been there. You are intrigued, but really don't know how much to believe of the fantastic stories you've heard. You want to see for yourself, but you're lost. Where do you go to find that infamous "Cathouse Experience"?

Sisters of the Heart

You expect them to be right there, close by, but where are they! You're embarrassed and don't know who to ask. You cautiously try the bell captain, the valet, the person on the street passing out x-rated flyers -- anyone! You even try the telephone yellow pages. Help! No one seems to know or want to tell you where they are. What now?

Feeling frisky, daring, adventuresome, looking for a little zest and spice, you decide to go to one of the many elegant top-less bars, or nude clubs in town. You have a great time with those renowned gorgeous Showgirls walking around with very little on but a smile. They dance close to you, seductively entic-ing the dollars out of your pocket. It's a wonderful titillating experience, but not quite what you had in mind this time.

You cautiously ask the cocktail waitress working at the club, or you approach the man at the door with your Brothel inquiries, but they seem oblivious to your request and try to dis-suade you from pursuing that route any further. This is quite understandable since these establishments want to keep your dollar in their pocket.

So you leave the Club, by this time really "hot and horny". You walk up to the friendly looking limo driver named Bill, who happens to be standing right outside the door. You brazenly ask him if he knows about the Brothels around here. A knowing smile slowly comes over his face. Not only does he know how to get there, but he offers to take you and be your personal tour guide! Great! Bingo! At last you're on your way.

The excitement is building as Bill heads out of town. You're truly feeling like a jet setting playboy in the long stretch limo, luxuriating in the back, maybe having a cocktail or two while asking Bill all your questions -- "Are the girls pretty? How many girls are there? How much does it cost? What's going to happen when I get there?"

He begins to describe some of the girls - blondes, brunettes, redheads, with big boobs, and great smiles. You imagine yourself partying with them -- all night long having them cater to your every wish and desire.

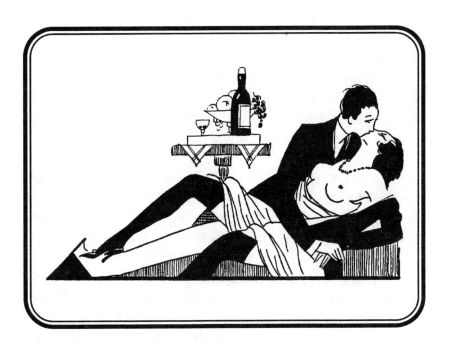

"You imagine yourself partying
--all night long

Sisters of the Heart

Your mind is racing, wildly fantasizing, picturing all these girls running around naked, well at least with erotic lingerie. You expect all the girls you've seen on adult video's and in Penthouse to pop out of the pages and be waiting for you behind those closed doors, seductively greeting you as you walk inside, enveloping you with their sexuality, coyly luring you into their boudoir, and then passionately catering to your every pleasure -- with their wet lips and tight pussy's doing all those things you've been reading about and hearing for years. It will be like you are starring in your own personal "x-rated" video! You look back at the bright lights of the city's horizon as it slowly fades from view.

You look ahead and see nothing but the endless blackness of the desert night. Bill assures you that you're almost there. The tension mounts. You begin to see some lights up ahead. Great. It must be a town!

You turn down a road just outside of town, but can't see the end of it. Again you keep driving and driving. All of a sudden there are these inviting signs saying "Straight Ahead. Keep on Cumming. You're On the Right Road To The Ranch."

Bright lights start to appear in the distance. As you get closer you see huge neon signs with flashing lights. Several wonderful mysterious houses line both sides of the road. Some have imposing barbed wire fences surrounding them with locked gates, while others have trees and grass with elegant facades and signs saying "Welcome. You're Here".

The Brothel Bible

At The Brothel Doorstep

Bill directs you to his favorite house. You are relieved because you are awestruck and absolutely overwhelmed with so many choices. He assures you that it really doesn't matter which house you go to, it's the girl you pick that will make your stay memorable.

You are reeling in dizzy breathless anticipation by now, as you stand at the front door ringing the bell. You can't believe this is happening! You're here! A beautiful woman opens the door and a whole new wonderful world slowly starts to unfold before your very eyes, as you step inside the "Magic Kingdom of Brotheldom".

*Inside the "Magic Kingdom
of Brotheldom"*

CHAPTER TWO

Brotheldom

Brothels are only allowed to exist, legally in Nevada, "out in the sticks", or in very small towns far away from the large metropolitan areas. These remote locations always make it very difficult for customers to find. Of course this helps to perpetuate and continue the mystery and mystique surrounding this profession.

The "mystique" also seems to come from the fact that the Brotheldom World is a very closed Society. Not many people in the Industry tell outsiders what really goes on behind those closed "Cathouse" doors.

Inside Brotheldom

Yes, there are drugs and alcohol. Yes, there is lying cheating, stealing, back-stabbing, cat-fights, pimps, and wife-

7

in-laws. Yes, there is stashing of money. All this goes on inside the Brotheldom World.

We were often times locked up in houses with sealed up and boarded windows, with no fresh air circulating or daylight allowed, with walls and carpets that had been ingrained with dirt from years of use. Imprisoned, by choice, for weeks at a time. On the other hand, some houses were extremely elaborate and elegantly decorated.

A Real Classy Place

One house where I worked had an enormous parlor where the customers would enter. It must have been 30-50 feet long and 20-30 feet wide with a ceiling of at least 20 feet. There were red velvet floor length drapes, red carpet, white and red leather furniture, glass and brass tables, a white baby grand piano on a raised stage under a magnificent tiffany chandelier!

There were two wings of rooms for the girls at this house. One wing had all white lacquer furniture with brass trim, long blue velvet curtains with adjoining bathrooms. All eight rooms were uniformly furnished, mostly the exact same size.

The other wing was older with wood paneling and furniture. Girls were allowed to decorate these older rooms any way they pleased -- from furniture to wall hangings.

8

The Brothel Bible

Double-Wide Trailers

One ranch where I worked had double-wide trailers hooked together out in the middle of the desert. There were no trees around, only little baby ones about 12" high, just recently planted. There were glaring neon lights, that would blare out in the darkness of night, and big flood lights way up high and huge "tacky" signs with arrows flashing and pointing the way inside -- "Visa and MasterCard Accepted."

Another Ranch

At another house there were no windows. We would literally be locked inside for three week periods at a time, then we would get 10 days off. We'd be "let out" until 3 P.M. everyday in a fenced yard out back and allowed to sit or walk around in a 20 x 30 foot square with a little side walk and paved area.

It always made me feel like I was a dog being "let out" to walk! I would frantically and desperately pace back and forth in that little yard for 30 minutes each day to try to maintain my sanity and get some exercise and sunlight and remind myself that there really was another world out there.

House Family Areas

There is usually a den/common area where the girls relax, watch TV, movies, talk and lounge around inbetween customers.

Sisters of the Heart

Some Houses have pools and back yards where girls can exercise or get fresh air and tans to maintain their healthy "look". There are sometimes dogs or cats running around inside and out.

There is a kitchen/dining area where girls can get food

"A Sister relaxing"

at all hours of the night. Usually cooks prepare the meals, but often times there are pantries where snack foods can be grabbed on busy days. Some houses have dining rooms with formal sit down dinners for the whole house and do not allow line ups for customers during the meal time. Some meals are gourmet, while at other houses, it's not much better than the City Soup Line, and then again some houses have no cooks, and you must "fend" for yourself.

Some houses let girls bring their own specialty or diet foods, and even allow girls to prepare their own meals during certain hours. Some houses would charge outrageous prices for food always priced ala carte -- up to $5 for a package of frozen brocolli! Then there was very little room to save leftovers, so if you didn't eat it all you had to throw the rest away.

There is usually an office where the owners, shift managers, and hostesses hang out, and all "behind the scenes" business takes place. All of these areas are strictly "off limits" to customers.

Customer Facilities

Depending on what house you are visiting, you may have to go through a series of locked gates before actually getting to the front door. You press buttons and bells, then someone inside buzzes the door open. It closes behind you. You walk on a sidewalk up to the front door. There is usually a Hostess at the door greeting you -- some are very friendly and warm, young and beautiful, while others are matronly and stern. This Hostess is not the Madame. She is most likely the Shift Manager. The owners are usually hidden away, sight unseen, and can be either men or women, or even corporations, but you probably won't be bumping into them. Be assured though, they are not far away. This is a very big money business and they keep a tight reign over their flocks.

Sisters of the Heart

How the owners and management treat the girls is often reflected in the atmosphere of the house. You can feel a warm, relaxed energy when there is harmony present in a house, or you can feel a coldness, hostility and tension when owners or management are more uncaring or calculating and treat the girls less humanely.

Once inside, you have your choice of going into a bar and/or parlor area. There may be girls in the bar talking with other gentlemen, or you may have entered an empty parlor, which resembles a living room.

In the Bar

If you are in a house that allows girls in the bar you can sit anywhere you like and talk to any of the girls present. You can approach the girls directly or you can just have a seat and sip a drink and talk to the bartender. But pretty soon you're going to have girls all over you, fighting over you, sizing you up, warming you up, feeling you out to see how much money you may be willing to part with, in other words, "hustling" you. Remember. This is our job. But "how we do it can make all the difference in the world.

All working ladies have the same goal -- to get you to spend the most money possible to have sex with them, but each girl's approach is as different as their sizes, shapes and personalities. Some girls worked well in that type of situation -- usually girls that were more aggressive.

12

Girls working in these "bar type" situations had to be up and in the bar talking to customers for their whole shift. Where as girls in other houses, where they weren't allowed in the bar area, would be able to sleep inbetween each customer or line-up, or do whatever they wanted.

Guys quite often, seemed to enjoy being able to talk to girls before making a selection. When you feel good about a woman you are talking with and she intrigues or excites you, for whatever reason, you can ask to go to her room and talk about parties and prices. However, if you've spent 10-20 minutes and still don't see a particular girl that strikes your fancy, you can let the Bartender or Hostess know when you are ready to be introduced formally to the ladies at a line up.

In The Parlor

If you have entered a house where girls are not allowed in the bar area, you will have a choice, you can either go into the bar, have a few drinks and then let the Hostess or Bartender know when you're ready to see the girls, or you can see the girls immediately.

The Hostess on duty will usually ask you which you would prefer. At any time, you can ask the Hostess or Bartender any other questions you may have. If you have arrived by taxi or limo, your driver will have entered the Brothel with you and usually be waiting for you in the bar. You can also ask him any questions you may have. He is usually well informed and can be of great service.

Sisters of the Heart

A lot of customers are so nervous when they get to the Brothel, that they keep drinking to get their nerve up to see a girl. If you are someone who likes to drink a lot before you party, take care. We've seen time and time again, the customer that can't "get it up" simply because of too much alcohol or drugs. We are not magicians. We do know a lot of tricks, but think twice before drinking too much. We want you to "cum" as badly as you do!

Line-Ups

In each establishment there is always some kind of "line-up" with girls standing before one or more customers. There can be anywhere from one to sixty girls lining up before you -- depending on the house, the shift, and the season.

In all of the houses where I've worked, the customers would sit on sofas in a dimly lit living room area. Lights were always as low as possible to be most flattering to our imperfections. The girls would wait in their rooms to be called out, or line-up in hallways, unseen by customers, and then march out in a long line and stop in front of the gentlemen waiting and introduce themselves one at a time.

Girls were not allowed to talk, laugh or giggle while coming out from the hallways or while standing in front of the customers. We had to stand a certain way, with our hands behind our backs, or folded in front, or by our side, with legs together. We couldn't move in line-up because it might draw attention to a particular girl and give her an unfair advantage over the other girls. Each girl, in turn would say her name,

"A Girl dirty hustling in a line-up"

nothing more. All private parts must be covered at all times (nipples and pubic hair). It was absolutely taboo and called "Dirty Hustling" if a girl broke any of these rules during line-ups.

Then, the customer would be asked to pick a girl. You can't talk to the girls during a line-up. All questions are handled in the privacy of the girl's room. The girl you choose, then takes you to her room to negotiate activities and prices.

*"So you think all girls who work
in Brothels look like this?
You'd be surprised!"*

16

CHAPTER THREE

What Kind of Girls Work In Brothels

You might think that there would be a bunch of "low-life slutty" girls working in Brothels. Kind of like those you see in the red light district of any big city, standing on street corners, leaning up against telephone poles, and doorways, lurking in dark alleys. But, you know what -- you'd be surprised!

Society has "branded" working girls as "bad". There is this underlying illusion, that if girl works for a living as a prostitute then she's not a "nice girl", she's unclean, she's really messed up emotionally, or she must have been an abused child. People tend to feel sorry for us and wonder -- "Can't she find a REAL job?"

Some houses were half-way houses for many girls (at least that was the position of some of the Management). They would reason, that if the girls weren't locked up in Brothels, they would either be drunk, on drugs, in the streets, or in jail.

I heard stories that one Brothel Owner would let girls come back to work, even if they'd been rowdy before, been on drugs or drank too much, because he knew the alternatives for the girls were even less desirable. He would kindly take these girls into his house, putting them in locked up conditions to make money for him. This owner was a very clever business-man. He was making tons of money off the girls he housed (or imprisoned), but this seems kind of a twisted compassion.

Brothels are not filled with unruly waifs that have nowhere else to go and nothing better to do with their lives. There are some girls like that yes, but very few. We are people. We are human just like you. We have feelings, emotions and families. We grew up in rich, middle class and poor neighbor-hoods. We come from all "walks of life". We arrive in Nevada from all over the world. We come for the money, the excite-ment and glamour -- just like you do.

We are girls and women that run the spectrum of all ages, shapes, sizes, nationalities, races and religions -- from 18 to 60 years old. Yes. We get face lifts, boob jobs, tummy tucks, lipsosuction, hair extensions, permanent make-up, cheek and lip implants to keep working as long as possible.

Being the most attractive lady in the house does not necessarily mean that you will be the busiest. Just as most people would not want to exist on a diet solely made up of one food or another, neither do men want to have sex with just one type of woman. Often times the prettiest girl in the house would not be picked, even if she had a warm and friendly smile, while the "Plain Janes" would get picked over and over again.

Men, we surmised, (just as in the outside world) were often intimidated by the Playboy model types, and more comfortable with the average beauties. We have found the male sexual appetite to be extremely diverse and strongly influenced by culture and society.

Why Girls Work In Brothels

Some of us are here to earn extra money -- to afford luxuries, like going to school, or getting out of "financial holes" we've dug ourselves into, or saving for the future, or just to make lots of money to spend and have a "good time", or to support drug habits, or to finance a new business venture, or to keep "pimps" in the styles to which they are accustomed.

We work here for many different reasons -- but it usually comes down to the fact that we make the most money in the least amount of time -- safely. This is not to say that the work we do here is any less stressful than your normal 9-5 job. The time we do spend working is extremely wearing and tearing on our bodies, hearts, minds, emotions, and souls.

Yes, we can make our own working schedules, taking as much time off as we want. We usually come back when our money runs out! We have to spend enormous amounts of time and money tending to our bodies and personal appearance -- to keep up the illusion of beauty and sex appeal as best we can.

Sisters of the Heart

It's very difficult to find comparable flexible working schedules anywhere else that even come close, unless you have your own business with other people running it for you!

We do get "hooked" on the money part. We do make money, lots and lots of money. We get so used to making lots, having lots, spending lots, that we get "stuck" in this cycle. The mere thought of a regular "9-5" everyday job, just doesn't seem to "cut it". A normal job seems so rigid and regimented after having one to two weeks off every month and being so "free-wheeling" (when we are on vacation and not at the Ranches working).

It becomes extremely difficult to even envision ourselves in any other working situation (especially at a much lower pay rate than we grow accustomed to).

Captive Male Audience

I admit, I must also have needed the attention from a "captive male audience". I must have had some ingrained female need to be reassured that I was still attractive to the opposite sex -- that I was sensual and sexy and desirable.

I think all women of all ages (maybe I should say "most") like to get dressed-up and look pretty and have men look at them -- isn't that an innate part of our species and a fact that has become a part of our cultural conditining, repeated over and over through TV, media, magazines and movies? I'm vulnerable. I've fallen for it's entangling, enticing allure. But I never had anywhere to go once I got dressed-up! I never had money to take myself anywhere, or was never with men who had money or any desire to go to "dress-up" places.

Even when we're happily married or with permanent mates -- every once in a while, when we hit low self-esteem points, for who know what reasons, we like to get dressed-up and get reassurance that, not only our devoted husbands or mates (who love us even with hot rollers in our hair, or when we first wake up in the morning in all of our puffy-eyed-no-make-up loveliness) are attracted to us, but there are others out there of the opposite sex that still find us attractive also.

We like reassurance that even if we were alone and independent in the world again -- we could still attract men. I never seem to lose that yearning. So, I guess, I arranged to have a place where I could do that and fulfill those urges.

Primping and Preening

I keep getting the image of the "Prima Donna" like strutting of male birds in the natural world with their beautiful feathers and such primping and preening around -- just because they have their beautiful plumage that attracts their female counterparts -- we women, yes, like to do the same. But, alas, in our "au natural" we don't have much luck -- we seem to be as plain as our sister female feathered friends are in the Bird Kingdom.

So, since we don't have it "in the raw", we have to try to manipulate our natural wonders into illusions of phenomenal splendor and lustful magnificence -- so enticing to our (already naturally handsome) male counterparts, that it "knocks their socks off". They totally fall "head over heels" for the gorgeous image we've concocted for that day of Primping and Preening.

They (the unsuspecting male) really have no idea what we go through for those illusionary effects (or what we really look like underneath all that make-up artistry, blow drying, curling irons, hot rollers, and carefully planned clothing, to emphasize the body contour that needs it the most and de-emphasize those that are imperfect) -- so we become a vision of heavenly magnitude for each unsuspecting male who happens to be so fortunate as to feast their eyes upon us and gaze into our purple colored contact lenses that day.

Emotionally Speaking

As working girls, we've experienced emotions that run the gamut of the spectrum scale -- from happy to sad, elated to depressed, disgusted to ecstatic, overwhelmed to wise. We're here to make money (for the most part anyway), but many of us have other emotional problems or hidden agendas, reasons for working -- to escape situations, reality, loneliness, etc.

There can also be compassion and camaraderie amongst the girls and management. It kind of feels like one big slumber party or a bunch of girls living together at a college dorm. The hostesses and managers become your family and you share intimate details of your life with them. The hostesses and managers are one of the only stabilizing elements in your life.

The Brothel Bible

Girls always come and go and flit around from house to house, wherever they think they can make the most money. So when you're locked in for weeks at a time the hostesses and managers are there five days a week and you see them as much, if not more than you might see your own family on the outside -- they become familiar and trust builds.

We often share our confidences and secrets with management before other working girls because so much jealousy and back-stabbing abounds. It is a very competitive business. If how much money you take home depends on how many customers you service, and the amount of money you can get out of them, as in any sales job, numbers work. The more times you get picked from line-up, the more chances you have of taking home a hefty paycheck. So you are obviously not thrilled when others get picked more than you. Besides just being a rejection thing, not enough money for mortgage payments, car payments, pimp payments, etc. have caused tears and breakdowns from many a girl.

Personal trials and tribulations of a working girl's life literally become "House" knowledge. All personal phone calls are usually made from pay phones located in offices or halls where other girls live, work and mingle. We all laugh, cry and feel what every girl in the house is going through, due to paper thin walls and management monitoring and eavesdropping in on phone calls at their whim.

Even customer negotiations are listened to by management through intercom's in every room! I have heard there are enclosed pay phone booths, which helps with the privacy issue at some houses.

Sisters of the Heart

A Safe Haven

Maybe I needed to be sheltered from the world for a while. Where does one go to be paid for being kind and generous? Where does one go to be paid for being themselves -- for showing compassion and caring for fellow human beings like one's self -- who are just trying to be happy from moment-to-moment, day-to-day, to find a safe spot where we can be ourselves without being judged, ridiculed, chastised, intimidated, put-down -- where there are no phony barriers or word games or hypocritical movements and gestures -- where people can openly and honestly say and feel what they want and need?

Sometimes, I start to wonder -- maybe I do function better institutionalized -- closed off from the outside world, in my own private fantasy land where I can do and say as I choose, and speak from my heart and touch and feel my humanness and not be stopped by mind barriers and should's and don'ts and all those other cultural conditionings, where the mind and logic take over for the heart and compassion.

Some of the Girls

Nanette

Nanette's is in her late 20's. She already has three children. Her husband works as an executive. They live about 10 hours from the Ranch. They have many expenses, as does any young family -- houses, cars, medical bills, etc., so they both work. He knows where she works. They talk to each other on the pay phone all the time. I heard they're getting divorced.

The Brothel Bible

Mercedes

Mercedes met her present boyfriend in a Brothel as a customer. She's been with him for about two years now. Mercedes already has two children, except she is only 24 years old. Her boyfriend visits her (as a customer) while she works. They talk on the phone constantly. He's about 15 years older than she is. They'll probably get married.

Sassy

Sassy was short and fat and very aggressive with the customers. They did what she wanted them to do. She was saving her money to go to college. She was a real trouble maker too, back-stabbing girls, trying to get them fired if they were making lots of money, so she would have less competition.

Jeanette

She was absolutely adorable -- tall, thin, short blonde hair, so shy she wouldn't even look at the customers in line-up (although I think that might have been an act to look so young and innocent). The guys ate it up. She could have easily been a model. She had that look -- very classy. She finally quit and went to live with a boyfriend, who she said didn't really like her.

Alexis

She was tall and big boned, fluctuating between a little overweight to a lot. She would sleep most of the time, and just get up for line-ups when she wanted to. She had a drug-using boyfriend who she gave all of her money to. She was trying to get rid of him (so she kept saying) but kept going back for more. She'd get caught up in the drug-using whirlwind. She was in her late 20's.

Laverne

Laverne was black and beautiful. I helped her glue her hair extensions on her cropped hair one day. She was 36, but looked like a 25 year old model. She had a lot of energy. I enjoyed talking to her. She had the same "spacey-fluid-energy" that I am attracted to in men. We would laugh and giggle. She was already a grandmother. Her phone conversations were always filled with problems about money back home and how they needed her to bail them out of whatever their current crisis was at the time.

Illiana

Illiana was a a very seductive South American woman. She led two separate lives -- her life at the Brothel and her life in the outside world. None of her friends, her husband or children knew of her secret life. She told them she was a traveling salesperson away on one to three week business trips. Her double life was a hard one to maintain -- the lies and coverups were quite an art. I was in awe of her capability to keep all her stories straight. She had a dignified, very professional appearance on the outside, with an elite group of friends. Her insatiable sexual appetite, on the other hand, was satisfied, and her spending money was constantly replenished with each trip to the Brothel.

The Brothel Bible

Sonja, Natalie and Brenda

These three girls were all in their early 20's with children. They rotated their working schedules, so that one could be home caring for the children and taking care of their shared Financial Advisor (that's the 90's label, I guess, for the old fashioned tried and true "Pimp"). I would overhear some of their phone conversations with their Financial Advisor and each other, and gained a new perspective on their lifestyle. They would laugh and be quite intimate. They would divide their daily living tasks amongst all four family members. It was quite a cooperative arrangement. I was really quite touched at the level of intimacy they shared -- something I had been trying to achieve in my own life.

Lily

Lily was an Oriental woman about 43 years old. She'd worked in New York City in this business and privately for a long time. She had also worked on a private house circuit, traveling from State to State, working in this profession, and had ended up in Nevada two years ago. She started supporting the Pizza delivery boy, giving him money and a place to live, so she had someone to be with on her time off. He used her and was seeing another woman. She would throw temper tantrums in the kitchen all the time -- screaming and talking so fast in her broken English. She was feeling desperate, because of her age -- wondering how much longer she could still attract customers and stay in this business.

Sisters of the Heart

Missy

I swear she was a man -- those big hands and legs, long arms, adam's apple and all that make up! Can they really make a man into a woman with a vagina and everything? I've heard they do a great job. It's still hard to believe. She/He's been here for a month and making more money than Lily! Can't guys tell!

I would bet my life Missy was a man -- very strange. Her girlfriend was here yesterday, cuz Missy moved in her own furniture, and they kissed! (I'll bet another transformed one, but I don't know which way). Later, my suspicions were confirmed when our House Manager saw her medical records. I must say I felt extremely uncomfortable when Missy was in the house -- strange energy.

Velvet

I met Velvet during my first year of working. I took a trip to South America with her to get my face lift, because she said it was cheaper down there and her Mom had it done there and looked great. So for me it was a very good deal, I was getting it done for one third of what it would have cost me in the United States and my girl friend was taking care of me at her beach house!

I never really got to know her until I went down to Venezuela. She started treating me like she's treated all the men in her life -- using them to get money out of them to pay her bills. She just didn't seem able to draw the line. And she was a fanatic about cleaning, which drove me up a wall. I couldn't even help her peel potatoes right! I had to just sit still on the couch while the maid was there, so I wouldn't dirty anything else.

Anyway, Velvet came back to the Brothel with me. She was so cheap that she got the handyman to buy her all her food, presents, supplies and things while she was there. I don't think she ever even had to service him or anything!

She never did understand why I never wanted to talk to her anymore when I got back to the U.S. and in my own private room, my safe haven at the Brothel. I was so glad that I was on my own again and not dependent on her in a foreign country with my head swollen and eyes shut from my face lift -- with no alternative but to live under her wrath and rule until I healed well enough to function again.

Melody

Melody was there when we got back to the Brothel. She must have been about 46 or 47, very pretty face, but the largest "pregnant-looking-stomach-but-she-wasn't" body. She was always wearing flowing negligee robes to cover her body. But she had a great knack for talking men out of lots of their money when she finally would get picked.

Brothel Attire

As working girls we could dress as sexy as we wanted (the sexier the better) without getting stares and snickers from the public and without being labeled as "girls looking for trouble" (as we would if we dressed like that outside our Brothel Domain). Girls, as well as customers, could live out their fantasies.

Sisters of the Heart

Some houses have strict dress codes -- lingerie during the day, long floor length evening gowns between 6 P.M. and Midnight, then nighttime lingerie after that. Other houses required that you buy the clothing they had for sale and wear pantyhose and red nail polish all the time. While other houses could care less, just as long as you made them money.

There were many traveling sales people that would arrive at the Brothel doorsteps at scheduled times, selling the girls Brothel clothes and jewelry. Usually the smart sales people would come on the day we got paid, before we'd spent all our money.

Generally you could wear almost anything you wanted, but absolutely no nipples or pubic hair could show. This was mandatory at all houses and seemed to be a Universal Brothel Code of Ethics.

I started out by wearing quite elaborate color coordinated expensive costumes with all kinds of feathers, flowers, lace, rhinestones, and assorted "doo-dads" -- anything to cover the imperfections of my aging physique. I wanted glitter and flash to draw attention to me in the line-up so that I could get picked. I wanted to sparkle and dazzle the guys -- so they would think they were "doing it" with a Showgirl.

Then, I saw one girl who just wore plain two piece bathing suits with no make-up, getting picked over and over again. I surmised that the more skin showing, the better. So I've pretty much adhered to that principle ever since.

30

The Brothel Bible

Some girls change clothes and hair do's constantly during the day -- when they don't get picked from one lin- up, they try something else. They spend hundreds and thousands of dollars on Brothel attire.

My Red Boots

Maybe I should write about my "Red Boots". I got this red vinyl, one-piece bathing suit-like costume that laced up the front. I loved it. So, I wanted red boots to go with it -- boots up to my hips -- I mean, long red vinyl boots with the highest spike heels I've ever worn that zipped all the way up.

So, a girl I worked with brought me the Frederick's Catalogue where she found some red boots for me for $187. So I debated and debated with myself and finally gave in. I ordered them, but they said it would take six to eight weeks for delivery! But when they arrived in two weeks I put them on and couldn't walk in the 6" spike heels! I couldn't even move-- the boots were so stiff! My knees were always bent, cuz they were so high. But I loved them. They looked "hot".

I finally decided to leave the in the office and put them on just before a line-up, much to the dissatisfaction of the other girls and hostesses who were always waiting for me to put on my red boots. I think everyone was glad when one of the heels broke -- but I got it fixed and I was very soon back in action again!

"Oh dear! I'm not getting picked in
line-ups. Should I change my hairdo?"

The Brothel Bible

Red Sequin Dress

We had nine girls in our line-up and it seemed that I was getting picked less on one trip so, I decided to make a red flashy, sequin, sparkling, see-through gown for night time. I got a red mesh dress and I sewed my sequins on it in strategic spots and put some red marabou on it too. Then I only wore it a couple of time and never got picked in it. I loved it.

So I proceeded to make another red sequin dress this time out of two yards of material from Wal Mart. I just sewed the whole piece onto a corset without even cutting it. I just kept sewing and pinning it together. This one really worked. But the sequins kept falling off all over the house. I left a trail behind me wherever I went. Management got so mad at me and started making me pick every sequin up. What a drag! But it was worth it for a while, cuz I made so much money in that dress. I finally got new sequin material where the sequins were sewed on, but it never seemed to hang as nicely as the Wal-Mart material. To complete my outfit I wore long red velvet gloves and red flowers in my hair -- obviously red is my favorite color.

Inside a Bordello Boudoir

Some rooms were very lavishly decorated -- satiny down-filled comforters with matching dust ruffles and soft fluffy throw pillows adorning the beds. The ladies personal taste in furnishings would be reflected in the decor of her room, including pictures of family members and loved ones sitting on top of dressers or hanging from walls.

Sisters of the Heart

You would sometimes feel as if you were walking into a pleasure palace, or even your own cozy little bedroom at home. On the other hand, you might also walk into a room and only see a barren bed, a night stand and very little else.

Sometimes, I would decorate my room by putting all of my costumes up on the walls instead of pictures. It seemed to get the men "hot" when they would enter the room, just by looking at my walls!

CHAPTER FOUR

How I Treat Each Customer

Maybe, I should tell you how I treat each customer. I'll go through the typical thing I do with everybody, cause it's down to a pattern with me, by now. But do keep in mind that every girl works differently. Each girl has her own unique routine she's worked out once she gets you behind those closed bedroom doors.

When a customer chooses me from the line-up and gets up from his chair to accompany me to my room to talk about types of parties and prices, I start talking to him. I ask him his name, as we're walking down the hall. I keep turning around, trying to make eye contact and to get him to talk to me. I figure the more he talks, the more comfortable he is, then, the more he trusts me, and (more importantly, the more money he spends). I try to get a lot of information out of him. I ask lots of questions -- to get to know as much as I can and keep him talking.

Sisters of the Heart

"Are you visiting from out of town? Do you live here? How long do you plan to stay here? Are you here on business or pleasure?"

"Okay, this is my room. Have a seat." They sit on the bed or in the chair. "Have you ever been out here before? It's kind of like an adult candy store -- the girls line-up, and you get to pick one, any one!"

"This is my room. I stay here 24 hours a day, seven days a week. I usually work for one or two weeks at a time and then get a week or two off."

"Let me tell you a little bit about the way we work here. We each work independently. We're all separate from each other. We go to the doctor's once a week. We're very regulated and controlled by the state. They're very strict with us."

Menus

"I have a menu here that describes some of the activities and things we can do. You can ask me questions." They look at my menu. It lists activities and prices. I think it definitely makes a big difference to have a printed menu that really looks like a restaurant menu. I made a lot more money when I started using menus.

Sometimes a customer would just read a price and say, "I'll take that activity" and just pay the price printed without even negotiating or asking any questions -- the dream customer. But, usually they try to haggle and negotiate.

The Brothel Bible

The menu I used had all kinds of descriptive words and activities that were to "whet" their appetite and get their juices flowing, their "dicks" hard and their imaginations running wild with anticipation, so they would pull money out of their pockets without thinking about it too much -- an emotional sale. (I have included a very subdued menu for an example in this book minus the graphic details to not offend those faint at heart

They start getting really "turned on" thinking about all the different kinds of things they can do -- every fantasy they've ever wanted to live out, I'm sure, comes to mind.

If they start complaining too much about the prices (my basic package started at $500) and it looks as if they are ready to bolt up off the bed and leave, I say, "Well, it's your first time here. You didn't really know what to expect. You had no idea. So, I have an 'Introductory Special'. If you tell me your budget, then we can limit the amount of time on any of the packages." I'm still trying to feel them out, to see how much money they have or want to spend.

My First Menu

My vagina had gotten so swollen one week, that our Madame (or head Hostess) finally understood that I didn't know how to negotiate for very much money and I was having too many customers for too little money. It was painful to touch for two days, until the swelling went down. I put tea on it, then a girl gave me vegetable glycerin too. So I would alternate between the tea and glycerin. Then someone told me to put alcohol on it -- I only tried that remedy once, diluted in water -- but something seemed awfully strong about that one.

The conclusion was that I was being too easy. I'd just tell the customers, "I'm your Barbie Doll and you get to do whatever you want. You direct the show." I'd limit the amount of time they could stay and "USE ME" by how much money they had to spend. Our Madame thought my methods were not working out too well so she directed me to a couple of girls who had worked in the "big money" houses before. They had written something called a "Menu", which listed activities and prices that they used during their negotiations.

So I took lessons from these girls after I'd made a feeble attempt to draft my own menu, which our Madame thought was still giving the store away.

So the pros shared their personal menus with me, and then I revised their ideas by doing some art work for them, and made it into a brochure instead of a one page typed piece of paper. I cut out some art work from the telephone book, put some laminating sheets on top of each pages -- and presto -- it looked like pretty slick stuff -- quite impressive, if I don't say so myself -- almost like a real restaurant menu.

Boy did I start to notice a big difference in that first week of using my "new menu". I immediately started booking much higher numbers, because I wouldn't have to do any talking (I'm not a hustler at heart). The customers often would just read the printed price and pay it without even asking any questions. Usually they would try to negotiate. But lots of times, they just took the printed prices as the final "gospel truth".

"Negotiating -- striking a deal"

Sisters of the Heart

Getting The Money

If we strike a deal and agree on a price for certain activities that are mutually agreeable to both of us, I tell them they need to give me the money so I can take it up front and let them know what we're going to be doing and for how long. I tell them we take credit cards, and we have an ATM machine. We also take cash and traveler's checks, and are very careful what it says on the credit card slip. Each house uses some kind of second company name that sounds like a (non-sex) business, like it could be a motel, or resort, or a consulting service.

I take the money or credit card (and driver's license, if it's a credit card or traveler's check) and put it on the dresser. I then tell them, "We need to do a little check first", as I lead them into the bathroom. I tell them that this is all part of our rules.

Next, I ask them to take their pants down. I get a paper towel and put some hot water on it (many girls use betadine, plastic gloves and 200 watt light bulbs to do this inspection), and then, gently wash their penis, checking for any open sores, bumps, anything unusual. 99 times out of 100 I tell them, "You're fine. You can put your pants on now. That wasn't too bad was it?" I say as I walk out of the bathroom.

If there is any problem, or any question about anything strange on a customer, we get a second opinion from another girl -- it's called a D.C., which I guess stands for "Double Check" or "Dick Check". A customer is politely asked to leave if there is even the remotest chance that something might be medically wrong.

After the check in the bathroom, they are usually stum-

Brothel Menu

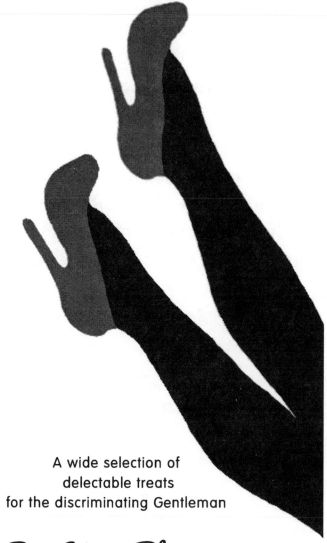

A wide selection of
delectable treats
for the discriminating Gentleman

For Your Pleasure

Brothel Ranch

Hi, welcome to our legal licensed Brothel. This is our menu which describes your every fantasy so we can make those dreams come true, call us for the friendliest and most attractive young ladies anywhere.

Also, for your convenience, we have a complimentary limousine service to the ranch. Pick Up and return to your hotel. 24 hour service.

We accept Visa and Master Card

CALL US ANYTIME

Come Join Us For the

"Time of Your Life!"

WARM UPS

* SENSUAL MASSAGE

* FASHION SHOW

* PARTY STARTER

* VIBRATE

READY, OK

* MISSIONARY
* LAY BACK
* HALF & HALF
* REVERSE IT
* ON YOUR KNEES

WARM UPS

1. **SENSUAL MASSAGE:** UNWIND AND RELAX WITH A LOTION OR OIL MASSAGE..

2. **FASHION SHOW:** OUR LADY WILL MODEL SEXY LINGERIE, STOCKINGS, GARTER BELTS, PANTIES OR YOUR FAVORITE FASHIONS.

3. **PARTY STARTER:** HER EXPERT HANDS WILL BRING YOU TO A FULL ERECTION AND/OR HER MOUTH WILL WARM YOU UP.

4. **VIBRATE:** A VIBRATOR BRINGS LOTS OF FUN TO ANY PARTY.

READY, OK

5. **MISSIONARY:** CONVENTIONAL SEX, YOU ON TOP.

6. **LAY BACK:** OUR LADY STRADDLES YOU, WATCH HER MOVE WITH YOU ON THE BOTTOM.

7. **HALF & HALF:** HER MOUTH GETS YOU HARD, INTERCOURSE BRINGS YOU TO A CLIMAX.

8. **REVERSE IT:** YOU START INSIDE, BEFORE YOU CUM SHE FINISHES YOU ORALLY.

9. **ON YOUR KNEES:** MOUNT HER FROM BEHIND AND CLIMAX INSIDE.

KEEP IT GOING

10. **JACUZZI PARTY:** RELAX IN YOUR OWN PRIVATE JACUZZI, INVITE ANOTHER LADY OR ANOTHER COUPLE.

11. **SHOW TIME** (2 GIRL SHOW): YOU WATCH WHILE TWO OF OUR BEAUTIFUL LADIES BRING PLEASURE TO ONE ANOTHER..

Keep It Going...

* JACUZZI PARTY
* SHOW TIME
  (2 GIRL SHOW)
* DOUBLE PLEASURE
  (2 GIRL PARTY)
* ORGY FANTASY

Cool Down

* SOFT MASSAGE
* REFRESHER

One Step Further

* DOMINANCE
* EXTEND IT
* BONDAGE
* FANTASY

12. **Double Pleasure** (2 girl party): Your needs are fulfilled by two of our ladies.

13. **Orgy Fantasy:** 2,3,4,5? Choose as many ladies as you like! Use your imagination.

ONE STEP FURTHER

14. **Dominance:** Submit, she's in charge.

15. **Extend It:** Stay overnight in the arms of a lovely lady. Breakfast in bed, multiple climaxes, champagne, jacuzzi, etc...

16. **Bondage:** Don't bother restraining yourself - she will do it for you!

17. **Fantasy:** You tell us.

COOL DOWN

18. **Soft Massage:** Bring your heart rate back down while our lady massages you.

19. **Refresher:** A nice warm shower finishes your evening.

Each lady is an independent
contractor, parties may vary
with different activities

METHODS OF PAYMENT

CASH
MASTER CARD
TRAVELERS CHECK
WITH PROPER I.D.

ALCOHOLIC BEVERAGES

DOMESTIC BEER
IMPORTS
WELL DRINKS
CALL DRINKS
WINE BY GLASS
BOTTLE OF WINE

PLEASE REMEMBER TO TIP THE HOSTESS

"Experience Your Wildest Fantasies" We'll Make Your Dreams Come True

Call

US

ANYTIME

Open 24 Hours

If you don't see your personal

preference listed,

do not hesitate to ask

bling over their feet, frantically trying to pull up their pants, which are usually down around their knees, as I go back into the bedroom to prepare the bed.

Preparing For The Act

I take a clean sheet out of a drawer, next to my bed and put it on top of the bed, and tell them they can get undressed and get comfortable and lie down while I'm out taking their money up front. I turn on some music on the cassette player, maybe give them x-rated magazines to read to keep them good and excited until I get back and turn down the lights to a soft red glow, as I walk out the door with their money or credit cards.

The management already knows how much money was negotiated because they listen to the discussions with the customer through the house intercom located in each girl's room -- just to make sure we bring up ALL the money the customer gave us. (If we can get away with it, believe me, we don't bring it all up).

Sometimes we had lookouts in the office to see if management was listening on the intercom to the negotiations. Then we'd tip the girl off as she walked down the hall to the office, and hand a few hundred, or whatever we thought we could get away with.

I would walk down to the office and give the money to the hostess on duty. I had to write down the time my party was starting, my name, my room number, the amount of money, and note if the customer was brought to the ranch in a taxi or limousine.

Sisters of the Heart

Undressing Me

When I get back to my room, I usually ask them if they would like to help me take off my clothes. They usually sit right up (if they're lying down). Then, they come to the edge of the bed or stand up to eagerly help me. Their hands are up and ready, fumbling, not knowing where to begin. I gently direct them, stand in front of them, with their face right at my breast level (if they are sitting down).

They take my dress off (if I have one on), then my bra gets unhooked (usually with much teen age like fumbling). My nipples are right there, gently grazing their faces. They are already getting a "hard-on" simply by undressing me! (Oh yes, I have calculated this).

So when they get my bra off, they usually start sucking my nipples or fondling my breasts (not all girls allow this, but if felt great to me). It's almost all over by then. I mean, their "dick" is usually sticking straight out at that point (in case there was any limpness at all left). I tell them there is more to take off, if they want to. So they help me take off my underwear. By now, they're touching my body everywhere.

Then, I stand them up -- and if they still have their pants on, I ask them if we should take them off. I undo them. Then I turn around, so that my bottom is right next to their penis. I wiggle around a lot, while I take their pants down -- first one leg, then the other, and their penis is pressing against my bottom. They love it. We do the same for the the underwear and socks -- slowly, sensually. If they have shoes on, I usually sit on their lap and take them off.

The Brothel Bible

In The Mirror

Then, I take their hands and tell them to come with me. I lead them to the mirror and stand them behind me, so we can see ourselves in the mirror. I put my arms up behind their head (so that my breasts look perfectly full and rounded). My bottom is pressing against their penis again. I'm wiggling and slithering up and down their body, smiling in the mirror and their hands are all over me.

They get really turned on looking in the mirror. It makes them feel as if they are watching themselves in an x-rated video or in a magazine. Boy, are they really hard and ready now!

Finally On The Bed

I ask them if they would like to lie down at that point. I lie next to them and gently stroke their penis and balls. I tell them that they get to direct me and tell me what they want me to do -- that way I don't have to figure out what they want, or try to second guess them. Everyone is so different, in what they like and don't like, and how they like it, and what turns them on, and how it's done and to what degree.

I put the condom on now, (a lot of girls are quite skillful at putting condoms on a guy using their mouth. They put the condom in their mouth and then, put it on the guy. I hear it's a real turn on -- I never quite learned that art) as long as they are nice and hard, I ask them if they would like me to use my mouth down there (meaning -- do they want me to give them a "blow job"). I do that for a while, and then ask them if they would like to be inside of me.

Sisters of the Heart

So I try to get them to be on top. I just lie there, with my legs up over my head. I feel that they have the most control in that position. If they still need more to "cum", I get them to try "Doggie Style". That usually does it (if they haven't come already by then). I just sit there, on all fours and they do all the work (in and out, pumping, pumping), they usually "cum" almost instantly in that position.

There are variations to the above -- sometimes they want me to be on top, or they have special little ways they like to try.

I give them a paper towel when they're finished to take their rubber off. Then give them another paper towel with water on it to clean themselves off. I go into the bathroom and clean myself also.

Most get dressed right away. Some lie there to recuperate for a moment. My timer (like a kitchen egg timer) has been set for the time agreed on. Sometimes, the timer goes off before we finish. If it still looks as if they might be longer -- I let them finish by "jacking" themselves off -- if it only looks like a couple of minutes more, I let them finish. Sometimes, they want to stay longer and they extend the party and give more money.

Customers Reflect Girl's Attitudes

In the beginning making love in the Brothel was just as warm, just as tender, just as fulfilling, as with any of my past or present lovers. IT WAS NO DIFFERENT! If someone would have told me that when I first started to work there four years ago, I would have told them they were crazy. I would never have predicted or dreamed that I could ever have felt this way. Whether this is the general rule with all girls -- I don't know. Maybe because at the beginning I gave out warmth and tenderness, that it came back to me, it was reflected. If other girls give out other vibrations, then that is what comes back to them.

I have observed that when girls are rude to customers, then the customers treat them accordingly. Sometimes girls got plenty of disgruntled customers, complaining as they would walk out the door demanding their money back.

Some girls are hard emotionally, because they have been doing this for so many years, they know no other alternative for making this much money. You can really get hooked into the kind of money we would make -- the money is very addicting. Being locked up is the price we paid -- self-imposed, voluntary prison.

Two Girl Parties

"Two Girl Parties" are where two girls cater to the needs of one man. Those were usually easy parties, cuz you'd have another girl helping you get the guy satisfied -- and the guy would usually be in ecstasy -- one girl using her mouth or making love while he was playing with the other girl. Four hands and two bodies on him all at once.

So many men would come in and say they'd been dreaming about this all their life. One very well-dressed man came in who wanted to do this for once in his life he said and he picked me. So I asked an older oriental woman to help me.

Sisters of the Heart

I specifically chose her because she really cared about giving the guy his money's worth.

So many of the girls just do "their time", cuz they already have the money up front and don't really put their whole heart into it. If I work with a girl with that kind of attitude (which is totally opposite to mine) -- I just kind of clam up. I usually get the guy to tell me how they like things done to them -- while other girls try to direct the whole show -- just doing what they know works. But I find each guy so different in what they like best and how they like it done that I ask each time.

Two Girl Shows

"Two Girl Shows", (as opposed to "Two Girl Parties") are where two girls each do each other and the men watch, and participate later if they have paid extra for that activity. Once we had eight very well-dressed Mexican business men show up one night wanting a "Two Girl Show". They wanted to work out a deal for the whole group of men and for all the girls in the house.

So somehow, I ended up being the spokesperson for all the girls -- even though I still pictured myself as the novice). So I kept going round and round with them for 30 minutes or so negotiating. We finally agreed on a "Two Girl Show" for 30 minutes for $800 with all eight men watching at the same time. Then, after the show, they would supposedly each pair off with a girl in the house and go to a private room for a "one-on-one" session of whatever their little 'ole heart's desired (well, whatever the girl that they picked would agree to).

I didn't know that they had already been across the street to another house and had been quoted over $3,000 for the same thing! Some negotiator I am. I was furious at myself when I found that out later that night. I may have been there the longest, but I was still "Miss Simple Simon" when it came to negotiating -- not anywhere near what you'd call an experienced "street hustler".

Anyway, the men wanted Rosa (a young 21 year old girl) and I to do the "Two Girl Show". Oh Great! Rosa has never done this before, barely understood English and could hardly even speak it. I'd only done this type of show a few times myself -- totally acting each time, "winging it" and "faking it" every step of the way.

So we all pile into my bedroom (cuz it's the biggest). The guys are all around the double bed, some standing, some sitting on the floor or on chairs, and Rosa and I climb on the bed. So here we are lying next to each other, me and this 21 year old Spanish girl.

I kept whispering to her what to do next. We keep kissing and touching each other all over. I would guess this is what acting feels like. When I'd gotten my training from the more experienced "girls" of what to do for this type of Show they told me that if the guys insisted on having us "eat" each other, then you put one of your hands down there in front of your mouth and just kiss your own hand and the guys never know the difference, cuz it looks to them like you're really doing it.

So I'm trying to whisper all this to Rosa in my broken "Spanglish" -- while the guys are watching our every move --

and Rosa is trying to understand it all. Geez! What a circus. It really wasn't too bad though. The guys weren't too demanding. Towards the end, though, they were starting to creep closer and closer on the bed, leaning over us, but not touching.

We were lucky because eight in the room at one time could have really gotten out of hand. Many houses have strict rules about not having more men than women in the room at one time -- there can be more women than men, but not vice versa. After our 30 minute spectacle I guess they'd all gotten their "kicks" cuz they left without pairing off with any of the other girls in the house to privately do their thing. The girls in the rest of the house were "pissed"!

Changing Perceptions

Things change here so much, so rapidly. Two days ago I should have written on my paper when I was feeling it -- I was feeling like a nymphomaniac. I mean, really loving this job -- loving to be touched and having my whole body used. And then, two nights ago, early in the morning, I fell in love, or in infatuation again, twice in the same night! One after the other. But the second one more than the first. But the first one was a really fun one too -- totally drunk and really out of it, but he talked to my stuffed bear.

Boy is that where I'm vulnerable or what? Whoever can talk to my bear and play like a little kid with me -- I can fall for in a flat minute. But thank heavens, I'd been married to an alcoholic before (who used to also talk to me and my stuffed animals) so I could check myself with that one. And he was

43...just my age...and really throwing money around. But I knew better this time.

But it really made me glad to be locked up in here. Because I could safely play for an hour or two with these "crazily" wild alcoholics, and not get in trouble or emotionally involved beyond those few hours. Whereas, if I had been on the outside and had met one of these characters, I might have gotten involved for longer --hours, days, weeks, months, because they were so much fun! Am I screwed up or what? But I'm working on it.

CHAPTER FIVE

Brothel Clientele

Men arrive at the doorsteps of the Nevada Brothels from every state in the union, from Europe and Asia, and everywhere else inbetween. The countless men who have graced our abodes (and bods) range in age from 21 (that is, if they didn't have fake I.D.'s) to 90 years of age, and they come in all shapes and sizes.

There doesn't seem to be any "norm" that we could use to describe the "typical client" we've seen over the years, but there does seem to be a common denominator of loneliness and curiosity. This is not to say that a healthy sexual appetite hasn't brought in its fair share of customers also.

The girls who work in Brothels and the customers that visit are just like the people you meet and interact with everyday in your home town. Customers come from all walks of life -- from politicians and doctors to laborers and drug dealers.

The Brothel Bible

Needless to say, we have serviced our fair share of the rich and famous. Some come from the most prominent and affluent of high society, whose names would be immediately identifiable if we were to put them into print. But to those past, present and future customers, we assure you, our lips are sealed. For once you step inside our World of Brotheldom your identity is hidden within our unspoken code of silence and ethics.

Young Studs

We get many young "studs" that just want to visit and try us out, for the "sport" of it! I call them "rabbits" because they do it hard and fast and just pound and pound as long as they can. There is virtually very little "love making" involved amongst this group. We think many of them are really oblivious to our desires. Although, there are those rare exceptions to every rule, and occasionally, a "naturally gifted young stud" appears without benefit of experience to knock us off our feet.

Older Clientele

It really is quite interesting to watch so many older gentlemen come in and pick the youngest looking girls. It's really a lot of work when they come in on their heart medicine and such things. It makes it very difficult to help them "get off" and we always worry about heart attacks at peak moments. Then there are those who have rods and pumps implanted in their penis so it always stays erect. Others come in with hand vacuum pumps and rings.

Sisters of the Heart

Curious Customers

Most men find out it's really a lot of fun, they get "hooked" and keep coming back for more! (Is that why girls are called "hookers"?) We call these men regulars. During slow seasons, we count on these "regulars" for our bread and butter!

Occasional Hunks

We have our fair share of "middle of the road" men -- not extremely handsome, yet not bottom of the barrel either. Occasionally, there have been those "drop dead" gorgeous, "stop-traffic looking" hunks that have arrived at our doorsteps -- the kind that makes you wonder if your make-up looks over-done, or not done enough, or if your "Right Guard" is holding up, etc.

If the "hunk" picks you, as his "Partner in Crime", you feel yourself getting those silly butterflies in the pit of your stomach (you know, the ones we feel when something really exciting or important is about to happen).

Sometimes, these individuals are as pleasant as they are attractive! But more often than not, they seem to feel that their physical attributes speak louder than words or actions. They act as if they are entitled to "preferential" treatment, accompanied by "preferential" rates!

When one of these extremely attractive customers tells us they've never paid for sex before, we have to bite our tongues not to laugh. Because we believe that most men realize they have always paid for sex one way or another.

The Brothel Bible

Believe it or not, we have had a handful of customers that would tell us we should be paying them! They had obviously forgotten who had picked whom from the line-up!

We normally feed their already "over inflated" egos by telling them it's easy to see why women would want to pay them, but since the "House" would not appreciate it if we started paying our customers we are required to collect for sexual activities.

The UnHunks

On the opposite end of the spectrum, we also had those that did not exactly fit into the "Hunk" category. Nine times out of ten, though, these men (the same ones we wouldn't give the time of day to in the real world if we met them on the street) often turned out to be extremely polite, mannerly, gentle, considerate and grateful for all of the attention we gave them.

Ralph

As a matter of fact, one of my most erotic sexual experiences, while in the Brothel business, was with one of these men. Let's say his name was Ralph (it wasn't, of course, but that sounds kind of fitting). Ralph was about 5' 9", weighed in at around 230 pounds, had very little hair remaining on his "too-small", pointed little head, bad teeth, and the remnants, of what I would assume, were horrible acne scars left from his youth.

"Ralph spoke with a lisp and wore
coke bottle glasses and was the
most 'well-versed' lover I
had ever been with -- bar none!"

The Brothel Bible

Ralph spoke with a lisp, and wore coke bottle glasses with black electrical tape holding his broken frames together. He did not make eye contact with me during the entire negotiation process. While he was being physically checked, he quivered and shook like a little puppy. This person truly was shaking in his shoes!

After returning to the room, once the money had been booked, I found him in the very same position that I had left him -- standing at the foot of the bed with his pants undone, his wobbly little legs looking unable to support his chubby frame, and his body language letting me know that he wanted to be anywhere in the world -- EXCEPT where he was! That wasn't going to be a problem, since he had only spent a whopping $150! He certainly wasn't going to be in my room for any length of time!

I instructed him to undress and lie down on the bed. Then, I proceeded to wash him, and laid down beside him. From that moment on, it was as if someone else had climbed into this person's body and totally taken over. To say that he became a man possessed, may be a bit of an exaggeration, so let's just say that he became a man with a mission. It was as if he needed to prove to himself, and to me, that he was a worthy opponent -- and that he did (thank you very much). HANDS DOWN!!

Where this person acquired his experience from is anyone's guess. Perhaps, he was, or had been, a "professional trick" (a man that frequents brothels almost as often as he changes clothes), or maybe, he had read every book ever written on the art of pleasing a woman, or possibly I had run into one of those rare individuals that just seemed to be naturally gifted and had always instinctively just known what made the opposite sex happy. In any event, this man was, by far, the most "well-versed" lover I had ever been with -- bar none! If you have any doubts in your mind, let's just say, this man was in my room for about two hours -- his $150 bought him more time than most of my $2,000 customers!

So, whenever you are out there, Ralph, my hat's still off to you. I get a twinkle in my eye, and a tingle in my $%#@ whenever I think of you. Here's a kiss meant only for you.

Men of All Nationalities

We would see men from around the world. Many of whom couldn't even speak English! At times, they had translators with them -- (tour guides, cab or limo drivers). It's really been quite interesting to see how "sex" is such a common language, bridging all cultural barriers -- all men seem to want it in pretty much the same standard ways whether red, black, blue, yellow, olive, tan, beige or white! It even made me feel somewhat like an ambassador of goodwill -- doing my part to bring the world closer together.

Asian Customers

We had a huge influx of Oriental customers. They seemed to be very excited just by the thought of being with an American woman. They would come in with their tour guides who would translate for them. In line-ups they seemed to always pick short, small girls. Once we got them in our rooms, the tour guides would run around from room to room and translate for them, or we would attempt to communicate in broken sign language (as we did with many of our foreign customers).

The house had some menus printed in Japanese, but I never used them because they seemed to have a lot of fancy words to describe parties like a "Kahlua and Creme Conquest" or a "Creme de Frappe Party". Now, how do you translate a party in English (let alone another language) which includes Kahlua and Creme applied to the genitals and then seductively devoured by the tongue in long titilatting strokes?

So we usually ended up writing prices on scraps of paper, until we both agreed. They usually had large wads of money. They would spend between $200 to $2,000 for a party. But they'd only stay for five to twenty minutes in the room actually "getting laid" no matter how much they had paid! We loved them.

There were no frills, not much foreplay, it did not seem necessary for them. They'd just get it hard, so fast, stick it in and "Wham Bam", they would cum like clockwork. They were very clean and meticulous in their hygiene and always wanted to take showers after sex, spending a long time in the bathroom.

A visit to a Nevada Brothel and the conquest of an American woman seemed to be a highlight and mandatory part of their trip to America -- right up there with visiting the Statue of Liberty. And just as our Lady of Liberty stands waiting in welcome with torch lit and outstretched arm - so, we too, eagerly await our Eastern friends, lying seductively on our beds, with legs open wide and fires lit, welcoming their cumming.

Mexicans

Mexicans from down Tiajuana way usually did not have much money. They were mainly laborers. Very often they would come in directly from working in the fields with their day's pay in hand, expecting to get laid for $30 or less. That was a lot of money to them. Many times it was all they had. They were sometimes very shy during negotiations, yet bold and macho during the act.

On the other hand, the Mexican businessmen and drug dealers were more refined, polite and respectful. Occasionally the "hot blooded" Latin Lover would appear and live up to his world renowned reputation and be a wonderful divergence.

Indian and Middle Eastern Men

Middle Eastern men always wanted to bargain and negotiate, trying to "wheel and deal" with us and get "laid" for as little as possible. I always felt over powered by their presence, in more ways than one. Now, anytime I am around the aroma of curry, patchoulli oil, Indian spices or certain incense, I am reminded of my experiences with our Indian and Middle Eastern clients. The aroma of their culture always seemed to linger with us long after they had departed.

The Brothel Bible

Pvada

Let me tell you about Pvada. He was from New Delhi, a regular customer of mine and something like a guru, I guess. I read an article about him once in some New Age publication. He traveled around the world teaching about spiritual enlightenment, meditation and such. I think everyone on the outside thought he was celibate.

He wore long saffron colored clothing and insisted on taking off his sandals before entering the house. Pvada was a very humble and polite man. He always told me that I was a special child of God.

He would call me late at night and tell me his sexual escapades from the past, since I was the only one he could talk to outside of his spiritual followers who would have been appalled if they only knew. I'm sure he was jacking off while talking to me. I was fascinated by the secret life this guru led. I later heard that he used to come on to many of his women followers. What a mockery of spirituality. I miss him sometimes.

A German Gentleman

Erich was tall and thin, really kind of gangly, but we had this wonderful energy between us. When we first met he kept saying, "What kind of magic are you doing to me?" I enjoyed our encounters, even though he drank too much and did too much coke.

Sisters of the Heart

Erich had his own little Mafioso band of associates. He was a gambler in the Casino Black Books and banned from playing poker around the world. So, he used his expertise now to train assistants to play in his place. I think he still went under false identities and played as often as he could get away with.

I gained a new understanding and insight into the mafia type mentality and form of justice when Erich told me the story of how he had to discipline one of his assistants for stealing $6,000. Of course, Erich couldn't turn him over to the law or legally prosecute him. So, yes, he took him out in the desert on some lonely road, beat him up and then took his shoes, leaving him stranded in the scorching heat, miles from the nearest town.

Afro-American Clientele

Without a doubt, Black men, time and time again, proved to be mysterious and exciting, totally at ease and natural in the art of love making. Their bodies seemed to flow into a passionate rhythmic fluid movement. Why any girl would choose not to make love with a Black man was beyond me. But, nevertheless, many houses had "special" line-ups for Black gentlemen.

Some of the Black men obviously knew, especially if they had come in with a white companion. Of course, there were also "special" line-ups for Couples, 69 Parties, Dominance, Two Girl Parties and Two Girl Shows.

The Brothel Bible

A European Couple

A European couple came in once. He was a former rock musician and wanted his girlfriend to be with a woman. She seemed pretty reluctant, like she was just going along with it all, trying to please him. This was my first experience "Doing a Couple". The other girls in the house assured me they would guide me every step of the way and tell me what to do. So, I made the line-up and got picked. I was scared to death, but somehow I got them into the VIP room after agreeing on a party for $1,800 for an hour and a half.

I would leave the room every 10-15 minutes and get coaching from the girls in the house on what to do next. I put the couple in the bathtub together, had them "do" each other, give me a massage, had my "handy dandy" saran wrap ready to use for protection (a female condom) when he wanted her to go "down" on me. He joined in and came again.

Since this was my first sexual encounter with a woman, I felt very strange. It made me see what men must see and feel though, when making love with a woman. It gave me a new perspective.

Social Services Administrator

One customer was thin, smallish with a well-groomed beard, dark hair. He was a Social Services Administrator, somewhere back east. He said he was now in the planning end of it. He'd paid his dues being a case worker and then a Supervisor. He wanted a "Fantasy Session" for $750 for an hour and a half. So, I told him he could "make believe" I was his "Barbie Doll" and tell me what he wanted me to do and direct me (my classic line).

He asked what the limitations were -- what he could and couldn't do. So I told him -- nothing from behind, no kissing on the lips, condoms on at all times. He had on very thick glasses which he took off, but said he could see, just needed them for reading. So he directed me. I don't remember specifically anything else.

$1,000 and A Letter

There was a customer who paid $1,000 one night. He was from the Midwest. He'd beaten his wife for nine years, and she'd beaten him back for the same nine years. He was cute until he opened his mouth (his teeth were all disfigured) and then when told me about beating his wife, my interest disappeared. I forget if he was doing alcohol or drugs also.

He wanted advice, which I don't give unless I'm specifically asked for it. He wrote me a letter which I received a couple of weeks after he left the ranch. It was the nicest letter. It made me feel good that I'd made a difference in someone's life -- that I'd given him the strength to go on -- given him the courage, and a different way of looking at his situation -- of not trying to get revenge from his wife.

School Gardener

A school gardener came in from California late one night about 12:30 A.M. He said he was on his three week vacation, was lonely and just needed to hold me and cuddle, sex wasn't important. So he gave me $200 for 45 minutes, and another $200 for another 45 minutes, and then, $500 more after that to sleep until the morning.

He kept saying "I love you" every five seconds. He just kept holding me and caressing me all night. We both fell asleep a couple of times. He was so gentle and kept telling me over and over that I was the kindest, gentlest, sweetest person he'd ever met. I ate it up.

It's always nice for the ego and self-esteem, but, realistically, I know that men can say the darndest things when they have an erection. I was curious to see if he was going to do a complete "about face" after he finished (as I'd observed before on numerous occasions). He didn't -- just a very sweet, nice man, very appreciative of a warm, cuddly body. I didn't have to perform at all -- only once I sat on top of him, but he went soft rather rapidly. So he ended up taking care of himself twice during the night -- no work on my part.

The gardener was ready to marry me and give me the world on a gardener's salary. I guess he was 40 years old and had gone out a lot, but never found the right girl. I wish I could have relationships with nice men like he was, but I get bored so quickly.

Sisters of the Heart

Whenever I left the room to book more money, I would put my white stuffed bear cuddling up next to him, and tell him the bear would keep him company till I got back. I'd put the blanket up around his neck to keep him warm and cuddly while I was gone. I kept bringing him orange juice too. (When someone touches my heart, they get the bear treatment).

Suicide Customer

One day this guy came in -- he was a kid, about 28 years old, making two or three hundred thousand a year. He'd started some kind of business. He had his little wife, and his little kid. He thought everything was perfect. Then his wife took off with his best friend! He tried to commit suicide -- taking pills a month or so before. Now he was ready again. He had his pills in the car (so he said) -- a wandering zombie. He was frozen. He wouldn't talk.

It was early one Sunday morning. I felt like God had sent me this person -- like I was responsible. I mean, he was ready. He was so disillusioned. He'd worked hard. He had his life perfectly set -- and then she went off with his best friend! I tried to get him to talk. I tried to get him to open up -- to do something other than being so closed. He was closed.

Slowly, but surely I just got him to talk and talk and talk. I said anything I could think of. I didn't know what to say. We had a little sex and I just talked and kept trying to get him to loosen up. I hope I succeeded. I gave him the phone number of one of our Hostesses that lived close by a few blocks away incase he needed to go somewhere else after our session. He said he was going to play basketball. I did as much as I possibly could. God would have to do the rest.

Sometimes It's Even Fun!

One man, named Phil (who turned out to be a regular) used to drive all the way from California (4-5 hours) just to see me and then turn right around again and drive back. He was a writer. Nice, really nice, healthful body. Cute. Nice gray hair. Our bodies fit really good together. Just felt good. Touching and holding. Real good. it was a lot of fun each time he showed up.

He used to call me a "Goddess". Yes. Yes. I ate it up. Tell me more. It didn't even feel like work. It just felt like fun. he showed up quite regularly toward the end. His timing was uncanny the last few times. I was getting deeper and deeper into a depression, and he would show up and lift my spirits so I would soar again for a moment. I would be desperately needing love and fluidity. he brought me server books as presents -- very nice gesture. It touched my heart. He was like a gift himself each time, just his presence and being. I missed him.

The Philanthropist

Raymond was from a foreign country. He was a philanthropist who would spend his money around the world building Temples for some religion. I remember him reading to me from this big binder one day about his religion. He kept coming to see me, every day for a week. He was staying at a local motel.

I would keep him in my room for hours, just to have some company. He liked watching me sew.

But for all of his philosophical gentleness and "so-called" self-anointed saintliness and humanitarianism on the outside world -- he was very "rough" sexually. He would keep pushing my head down when I would give him a "blow job". To me, that is one of the most disrespectful things a guy can do to me (other than the obvious physical abuses).

One Of My First Customers -- Almost

My first or second day on the job, this guy named Dan came in and sat on the couch in our waiting room. I guess he was in his late 20's or mid 30's (who knows). Anyway, he worked for the telephone company and wanted me to leave with him, right then, and there, and supposedly live happily ever after....tra la la la..... He said he couldn't believe he met someone like in in a place like this (what an original line). He was very cute, though, short and little. He said he only had an ATM card or something. So, he left and went to a bank or a casino to try to get money. When he came back, he said it didn't work, so he had no money to party -- sounds like a right good prospect for marriage to me!

$2,000 Tip

A really nice man came in from Hong Kong and spent $1,000 and left another $2,000 as a tip. I carefully rolled up the $2,000 and secured it with a rubber and put it inside of two condoms and then up inside of my vagina so I wouldn't have to split it with the management. He was fun. He loved to sing Karaoke. He loves to sing for fun. He really only wanted a massage -- a Japanese massage. He told me that in a Japanese massage, they massage you with their body. So, I said I'd try.

We put lotion on. Then he said he liked powder. So we put powder on top of the lotion. Then, he went into the jacuzzi. He didn't really want to cum and he didn't. He was in a family run business. He worked all the time travelling -- some type of clothing designer who does trading in California. So his group decided to come over here, then they were going back to California. He put his face next to my hair. That was nice. It was only 15-20 minutes. That was it and he was gone.

Later, I took the "wad" (which was very large) out of the condom and it's secret hiding place and folded it neatly in half and put it into the empty film slot of my Polaroid camera and had a worker (unknowingly) deliver it to someone outside to deposit it in the bank for me. It was way too large to sit inside of me for very long. It hurt.

One time, when I had a smaller wad inside me, I was in the kitchen with a night shirt on and no underwear and the money-filled condom fell out while I was talking to one of our hostess-managers. She was so self-absorbed in her own conversation, that she didn't even notice as I non-chalantly bent over and scooped it up, ever so casually...Phew...What a close call

Sisters of the Heart

Lost Tooth While Blowing

Then there was one short, roly, poly little man with funny teeth. I'm so aware of people's teeth since I just had cosmetic veneers put on 16 of my teeth. And my first day back at work, one of the back veneers came off while I was giving a blow job. So I just calmly, secretively, put it in a kleenex on my night stand. Nothing else really significant about the roly poly man. I think he spent $100 for 15-20 minutes.

Stomping The Bed

The craziest man was the one who told me that he "gets off" if he can see someone stomp on little animals. I said I would not do that (as my stomach was turning over). But, my compromise was to stand up on the bed with my legs straddled over him and stomp on the bed instead. That had to be the "grossest" request I've ever had. It turns my stomach just to think that there really are human beings like that out there....

Richard, The Wild One

Richard came in that first year. He was from Chicago. He arrived at our doorstep in a taxi that had just driven him eight hours to get there. He hadn't slept for a couple of days and needed a bath. I had on my shorts and an old blue shirt and was ready to go out the door and do some errands in town, but he picked me anyway. (I was working at a house that actually allowed some time off in the morning to do errands).

So, I dumped him in the bathtub, shaved his beard, bathed him, gave him some vitamins and tea to calm him down. There was no "sex" and I got $600 for 30 minutes. The girls said that he came back later that day, but this time with no money. The taxi driver had left him on the corner. I guess he ran out of money and couldn't pay the taxi driver. I looked out the window when I got back from doing my errands and he was still standing there on the corner. Big heart that I have, I didn't invite him back in.

He came back a month or two later and said he'd been to the "dry out" clinic I'd recommended in Baja, Mexico to sober up. He kept calling me on the phone. He said he was trying to buy a Ranch. He kept inviting me back to Chicago to "hang out" with him and keep him company.

He was even crazier the second time he came to visit -- even higher on drugs than the first time. This time he chose two girls to cater to him at one time -- this is called a "Two Girl Party". I don't know what it was about him, but he made the biggest messes each time. He was so demanding of our attention every single second. He even got into a verbal fight with the other girl.

Disfigured Preacher's Son

A young man came to the door as a customer one day. He was tall and gangly in dirty clothes with half of his face disfigured (maybe from being burned). He used to live close by, in a small town many years ago and was a Preacher's son. He'd been living overseas recently, but still owned property in this desert town and was considering moving back.

Sisters of the Heart

This man was so non-aggressive and gentle -- an experience I never would have had in the outside world. I never would have even looked twice at this man. If I would have a bunch of regular customers like this man, maybe I never would have left this business. Where have I been all these years to have missed such gentle tenderness and passive encounters?

Bob, The Grandson

We met one night when he came in with his two bodyguards (the grandson of a multi-millionaire magnate). We had gone at it for four hours straight. My whole body had been throbbing the next day. When I do it so much, my body keeps throbbing and I want it more and more and more -- but I'm really so tired and my legs can't move -- yet my body's still throbbing.

He came back in the afternoon the next day and told me it had been the same for him too. The whole day long he kept thinking about me. You know, it was kind of nice. But we were both so tired and exhausted from the night before that he only stayed 15 minutes. We both couldn't hardly do anything.

He appeared to be pretty straight that next afternoon. I don't think he was doing drugs the next day. Bob was kind of conceited though -- in his early 20's. He had millions and would inherit millions more, but his parents still made him work everyday. He said our love making was better than with a fiance he used to have. He was sick after our first night four hour session. I guess he came down off his drugs during our four hour session.

The Brothel Bible

The Slow Talker

There was a nice, very unusual man one day. Two other girls had already been with him. They called him crazy, but I thought he was just unusual but very nice. He just talked very slowly. His body was long and lean -- he felt real good, physically. We felt like we were in love. He wanted to take me away (again for the umpteenth time). So many customers want to come in and whisk us away, becoming our rescuer, our knight in shining armour to live happily ever after WITH THEM.

He spent $1,000. Guess his Dad just gave him $90,000 and this other guy was supposed to give him more money and he was trying to figure out what to do with it all -- should he make a move, write science fiction, do remodeling? He didn't quite know what to do. I guess he was a Social Worker before and he got fired or something. He didn't have a home and would always come to the ranch in a taxi.

He was lost and lonely and wanted a woman. He wanted to take me away with him that day. I wouldn't do that. I let him stay six hours though. He should have only stayed four, but I let him stay six. I kept giving him coffee. He seemed really depressed when he came in, so my goal became to make him smile.

I realized that I didn't want to see him again. Then he became very obsessive, phone calls all the time. He made up stories and called the management trying to get through to me. He would tell them he wanted the house limousine to pick him up and bring him out to the ranch, but he needed to talk to me first. I just kept refusing to take any of his calls I told him if he wanted to talk, I would see him as a customer only.

Sisters of the Heart

He came out to the ranch and stayed 12 hours for $2,700. He brought me a wedding ring that he said he'd gotten at a pawn shop. He read me a three page letter -- a marriage proposal, and I was supposed to tell him, at the end of our session, if I wanted the ring or not. I didn't want to lead him on. I just tried to have a real good time while we were together (after all, he'd just spent $2,700!)

At the end of the session, I told him that I didn't want him to have any hopes or anything, because I couldn't accept the ring and I didn't want to marry him now or in the future. I tried to explain to him that here inside the house was an unreal world, and I wanted him to be happy in the real world.

We only made love once. We really just slept most of the time. I fed him dinner and coffee and pudding. We just slept. I was so tired. Just held each other. He smoked. He just kept talking and talking. He always wanted to talk about the future -- us being together. I kept telling him, just enjoy the moment, I didn't want to talk about the future. He tried to call a few times after that. He wanted me to keep the ring anyway. No. I couldn't do that.

Small, Medium and "Oh My God!"

I was so surprised when I'd get a very short skinny customer in my room. You couldn't tell anything about his physique with his pants on, but "Oh My God", when he pulled his pants down. I've seen some of the biggest "dicks" on the smallest men. It would look like it was just stuck there, like it didn't belong. Where did that thing come from?

How Big?

Sometimes really well-hung big guys were so huge that we'd have to turn them away! There would be no way we'd let that thing get inside of us.

Often times a guy would come in for a "Straight Lay", then during the medical check, he would turn out to be an "Oh My God". That mean way too big, even when he's not hard, for any of our precious money-making pussys. We would tell them, as politely as possible, that we couldn't service them.   If they would fit into our maxi-size condoms we would offer to give them a "Blow Job" or "Hand Job", otherwise, we had to take them back to the parlor and report the problem to the Shift Manager, who in turn, would escort them to the door.

How big is the biggest one I saw? Well, I'll tell you -- since you really want to know. I swear it was scary looking and he looked so unassuming. It was at least 10" long and that was SOFT! And about 5 to 6 inches around! Who knows how big it was when it was erect! I didn't hang around long enough to find out. One thing I do know for sure is that he had a big, big problem.

Introverted Dick

I swear some were so small they looked introverted -- especially when the man was extra heavy. I have so many memories of trying to pull this knob out -- like a small cupboard door knob -- trying to get it out a bit to get a condom on -- imagine your head down there holding a condom with both hands to keep it on, as you try to get your mouth close enough to give a "blow job". I often felt like I was being smothered by mountains of fat with my face buried deep between their legs.

CHAPTER SIX

Money Money Money

Being a Brothel Prostitute is an extremely lucrative business, but it is also very competitive. All girls, no matter how beautiful and alluring they may be, have to deal with a lot of rejection. But even if you are not picked all the time, in some very busy houses, you can still take home $2,000 to $4,000 a week. And if you are a "Top Booker" you could leave with $6,000-$8,000 a week and I have heard stories about much more than that.

The girls work as Independent Contractors. We pay for room and board anywhere from $20-$35 a day. Sometimes food would be sold separately and could run several hundred dollars a week just for meals.

We would split half of the money we "book" with the "House", including tips (although that varied from house to house). Then, when a taxi, limousine or airplane would bring customers out, we would have to give the drivers anywhere from 20% to 40% of the total money a customer pays before splitting with the house.

Sometimes we can supply our own "raincoats" (condoms), but sometimes the house required us to buy the Ranch condoms for upwards of $2.00 each! Houses would usually keep supplies of condoms in stock and sometimes lubricant too (KY Jelly and Astroglide).

We were always tipping hostesses to run to the store and buy us supplies, special foods, etc., to run various errands for us, since we were locked in. We usually tipped very well. They would make good money.

Stashing

All of our belongings were always searched when we would arrive at the house for our stay and again when we would leave. Supposedly, that was to keep illegal drugs out of the house, but the management was also looking for "stashed" cash (cash from customers pocketed by the girls and not reported to management). Even our outgoing mail had to be left unsealed and searched before closing!

Periodically we would have room searches, without notice. All girls would be called to the dining room, or parlor and management would go into the rooms and search for drugs or cash. Girls had ingenious places to stash cash -- mainly in vaginas -- but occasionally under rocks outside, in cars. Hostesses who had been working for years knew all the tricks -- light fixtures, air vents, hair spray cans, etc. so we were constantly dreaming up new places.

Even our car keys would have to be turned in to management. One girl told me a story about one house where management suspected a girl of stashing in her car. They went to her car, literally ripped it apart on the inside. You guessed it! They found it and the girl was fired on the spot.

At another house, one hostess suspected a couple of new girls were stashing on their second day in the house. She made the two girls strip down to their G-strings and turn around with their backs facing the hostess, then she asked them to bend over. This way any money stashed up inside their vagina would definitely show in this uncompromising position. Yes they were caught and fired.

We also heard stories about one hostess taking "kick backs" or payoffs for keeping the working girl's "stashed" cash! That whole house was "stashing", and getting very openly brazen about it.

If you could get more money out of the guys once they were in a party that was called "extending the party" or an "extension" (of course, that was when you booked the extra money with the management.) One girl who was an expert at this method (and never reported extensions) once only booked about $3000 for the week, but actually went home with $4,500 extra. She really was amazing, I still don't know how she did that!

Sisters of the Heart

Extension money was the easiest to stash, because management usually didn't listen in on your parties after the initial money had been booked. So it was easy to just keep that extension money and the management wouldn't be suspicious about anything, unless they asked the customer how much money they had spent while they were leaving. That was a calculated gamble each and every time.

And we could never "stash" if that customer had come in a taxi or limo, because the drivers were getting a "cut" of everything the customer spent, and they were thorough at grilling the customer after the party.

One time, my friend was leaving to go on her vacation, so she had her stashed cash in her wallet. I took it out and put it on top of the back tire of her car, which she could see from her window. When I came back inside to tell her where I put it, we looked outside and it was gone!

We couldn't believe it! We both panicked! She'd be fired if management found her wallet with that much cash in it! My friend was so "rattled" she just went in the shower and turned on the water. I calmed down and decided to go out for a morning walk to look for it. The dogs had carried it over by their dog dish. We were very lucky. I think we put it under a porch step after that in the front -- away from the dogs! We hugged each other while she was leaving and management was watching us, while I whispered in her ear, "under the porch". Phew what a close call.

The Brothel Bible

The Daily Brothel Grind

I would try to wake up and do things during the day as if it were any other normal day (as if I were outside the Brothel). I would putter around and do my everyday routine -- like exercise, getting dressed, putting on my make up, fixing my hair -- except I would put on sexy costumes, lingerie and evening gowns, instead of street clothes, and heavier make up and exaggerated hair styles, to stand out in dim red lights. Then, I would proceed to do business that needed attending to for the day, paying bills, etc., EXCEPT I couldn't leave the house.

Every once in a while (the frequency depended on the house you were working at) there would be a knock at the door or a doorbell ringing. These doorbell rings could be anywhere from screeching, obnoxious buzzers, to soft and melodic chimes. I used to awake in the middle of the night and sit up in bed, when I was on my vacation, thinking I was hearing Brothel bells (especially after leaving the screechy bell brothels!)

A customer would arrive and we would have a line up. If I was picked by the customer, I would have company for a while, and then, they would leave and I would continue with my day.

I would take many frequent naps to keep my strength up since I never really got any regular sleep hours. Customers could arrive at the door non-stop, 24 hours a day, seven days a week and we would have to always be ready, our physical appearance and our rooms neat and tidy.

Our sleep patterns changed radically. I used to sleep when I was tired, and force myself to sleep even when I was not, especially if I was anticipating many knocks on the door that night (like on a Friday or Saturday night).

One of the girl's favorite houses was owned by former working girls. They would allow the girls to be on shifts, so they could get a full 12 hours off each day and some uninterrupted sleep. They could stay at the house or go off the premises and stay at apartments during their 12 hours off each day. If they stayed at the house, they were awakened each morning with coffee brought to their room by a maid.

While other houses have sleep shifts where the girls who were the "Top Bookers" for that day could go to sleep at about 2 or 3 A.M. and not be required to be on the floor for line-ups until 12 or 6 P.M. The girls who didn't book as much money, had to keep dragging themselves up for line-ups all night long. They could usually go to sleep at noon, but would have to be ready by 6 P.M.

But at very busy houses, even if you were a "Top Booker" for that day, if taxis or limousines came in you had to get up, or if it got so busy that all the girls who weren't "Top Bookers" were busy, then the "Top Bookers" had to get up too.

I once worked in a house like that. It was so busy all day and night with an endless stream of customers. We had no sleep schedules, just work, work, work, until we collapsed like zombies from sleep depravation. When working in those places, it truly would resemble a "meat market" mentality. I've heard that place has changed their scheduling now to be more humane.

The Brothel Bible

The Time You Arrive Makes A Difference

So if you, as a customer, arrive at about 4 A.M. after partying in town, remember you may be seeing girls who have been catching "cat naps" inbetween customers or have just been allowed to start their eight hour sleep shift.

Or if you arrive at 11 A.M. the girls may just be getting up and in varying stages of getting ready. Be gentle, if you see girls in these varying stages of just being aroused out of sleep, or with only half of their make up on. If you're kind and a little patient, they will respond to your consideration. If you're demanding, irate or irritated that they are not wide awake, bushy tailed, perky and looking like a Playboy Model, they may respond likewise.

But for the most part you will be seeing girls, "hot and ready" for action. Remember that's why they are there - to make money!

Imprisoned

When we are locked up inside a Brothel, I can't begin to describe the changes we go through. Our emotions, and senses are so deprived. Our perception of the world, reality, the existence outside of Brotheldom are all askew. If we try to make any decisions while inside, they are almost always wrong, because we are in such an altered state of reality.

I always try to give myself at least a few days outside to regain my sleep and rest and my emotional sanity before I make any decisions. In reality it usually takes at least one month to get back to normal. We become so needy when locked up for 24 hours a day, without being able to run to a store or to visit with friends and relatives -- or simply to be touched or held by those we love.

Many girls also carry an extra burden of guilt when locked up -- and even when they're out because they lie to those they love about what they do for a living when they're gone for weeks at a time. Those girls have trouble when the doorbell rings and they are on the pay phone talking to a loved one. They sometimes try to muffle the outside bell sounds and girls chattering in the hallways, and customers leaving by holding a towel over the mouthpiece to block the sounds.

Some houses only allowed two phones a day -- a total of ten minutes each (that included incoming and outgoing combined!) And even those calls were in an office area where all employees and/or working girls could hear every word. To make matters even worse -- sometimes management would listen in on conversations from telephones hooked up for listening from other rooms.

There would absolutely be no privacy in those situations. Girls were also timed, down to the minute, each time they would get on the phone -- they would have to sign in and out. A couple of times, my calls were cut short, just because the management was picking on me.

The Brothel Bible

Sunday Visits

Different houses had different policies for allowing husbands, boyfriends, or friends to come and visit with the working girls -- "Visiting Hours".

One house had no visiting hours at all. In another one, we were allowed a one hour visit with people from the outside, between the hours of 10-12 in the morning on Sundays only -- and then only for one hour.

We would have to entertain our guests in the den (combination kitchen, dining room) sharing the space with whomever was in that room at the time (cooks, employees, girls, maintenance people, bartenders, etc.) -- again no privacy, whatsoever!

Some hostesses would let us use the parlor, every once in a while (when the "big boss" was not around). That was a much larger room and you could almost whisper and not be overheard. The boyfriends and husbands were absolutely banned from going back to a girl's room -- supposedly for medical, health, safety reasons (they didn't want us having unprotected sex, without being tested again). I think management was also suspicious of girls passing "stashed" cash out of the house, or drugs coming in from the outside.

A few times I actually had a friend come visit me. I would give him a list a couple of days before and he would bring me all kinds of presents and goodies from town -- little things that would just put a smile on my face and help make my stay a little more tolerable.

Sisters of the Heart

It was always wonderful to have someone come and visit you from the outside world -- I guess, it gave me hope that there was still another type of life out there -- that we really were different people on the outside -- with different feelings and emotions -- it was always a wonderful reminder.

But I started to understand why Brothels possibly acquired the label "Cat Houses". Girls can start to act like a bunch of "cats" on occasion, bickering, fighting, scratching, and clawing when living together 24 hours a day in such close confined quarters.

Medical Testing

We would have to be tested by the county for all types of Sexually Transmitted Diseases. We were required to go directly to the Ranch after completing the testing and sit there for two days locked up, waiting for the results. We were not allowed, by law, to work until we had been "cleared" by the county, meaning that we were free of all diseases. We had blood work and swabs and peeking and poking each time.

Once we were inside, then either private doctors would visit the houses once a week and test us again, or we would go out to a private clinic one day a week for testing. If we went outside we would usually be allowed to do some errands for a couple of hours with a chaperone. It was like heaven to be let out.

CHAPTER SEVEN

Questions Men Asked

The following questions were those most frequently asked by our customers over the years.

"Do You Live Here?"

This was the question most often asked. As has been explained in previous chapters, many working girl's rooms looked as if they could have been used as full page lay-outs for House Beautiful or Better Homes and Gardens.

Everything, and we do mean everything, in these rooms were designed to complement the over-all decor. Dust ruffles matched comforters, that matched lamps, that matched pillow shams, that matched bolsters, that matched draperies, etc.

Sisters of the Heart

These rooms were beautiful, inviting, and just waiting to be used as a pleasure palace. So it was conceivable that men visiting these rooms could feel anyone investing that much time, energy, and money on their surroundings might possibly live there full time.

But just as we have told you how beautifully and elaborately decorated some rooms were, there was also the flip side of the coin. Certain houses did not allow you the liberty of painting, carpeting, paneling or even adequately cleaning the room that was assigned to you.

These rooms were one step above a hovel (and sometimes that was a very small step!) The carpeting (if it could still be called that) was so worn and filthy from years of use and abuse, that it was flatter than linoleum. If you were so brazen as to walk on it shoeless, you were virtually taking your life into your own hands (or maybe we should say feet).

Windows to the girl's rooms were often nailed shut years ago. We could never quite figure out if this was done to keep customers out or girls in!

So, as you can see, the Brothels or Ranches where the girls were employed were as different, and sometimes unique, as the individuals that worked in them.

"Do You Like What You Do?

How could this question ever be answered with a simple yes or no? Does anyone ever LIKE their job all the time?

The Brothel Bible

Would you like to have the ability to make in excess of $150,000 per year?

Or be on call 24 hours a day, seven days a week and at the end of a particularly slow period, not even have enough money to pay your rent?

What if you had a gorgeous member of the opposite sex pay you upwards of $5,000 for one hour of your time, with nothing more involved, than intelligent conversation, and adult companionship?

Or would you like to spend that same amount of time grappling with a rowdy customer that reeks of alcohol and body sweat who violates not only your body, but your very soul?

Imagine having a wonderful, sensual, sexual fantasy unfold before your very eyes, with you being a more than willing participant?

Or to be propositioned, then expected to participate in a perversely "sick" sexual act, such as pretending that you are a 12 year old child that is about to be sodomized by their own Father?

Visualize setting your own work schedule, taking as few, or as many, days off each month as your little 'ole heart desires?

Or working for a company that requires you to work 21 days at a time, being on call 24 hours a day, during that time, and if a holiday such as Christmas or Easter falls within your three week "tour of duty", don't even THINK about asking for it off?

Sisters of the Heart

How about being able to surround yourself with friendly, outgoing, intelligent co-workers that share many of your same interests, hopes, dreams and goals, while living in a dormitory atmosphere?

Or try to co-exist with people for an extended period of time that you have absolutely nothing in common with that lie, cheat, steal, drink and do illegal drugs on a daily basis?

Fancy being secretly envied by other women because you are living out the fantasies they only dream about?

Or being dishonest with everyone that you know (outside of your work) about what you REALLY do for a living, because shame, pride, and fear of rejection or humiliation will not allow you to tell the truth?

Dream of making love with some of the most handsome, intelligent, sophisticated men on earth - such as a man who is instinctively attuned to your deepest secrets and desires, one who carries you far beyond the outer realms of physical lust and passion into the unfathomable depths of endless bliss.

Or having sex with someone that you've never met before (or would never want to meet again), feel no emotion towards, except contempt, and be required to act as if you are enjoying yourself, and then have to say thank you after the deed is done.

"How Many Customers Do You See A Day?"

The number of customers we saw each day varied as much

*"Dream of making love with some
of the most handsome, intelligent,
sophisticated men on earth....."*

as their shapes and sizes. Depending on the house you're were working at - there could be zero to three customers on a slow day, four to six was an average day, and up to twelve customers on a very busy day in a medium size house, while in a very busy house some girls could see up to 20 guys in a day.

On any given Friday or Saturday night you could find half the girls in the house sitting in their rooms, or in the Community Den area watching a two hour movie -- without being interrupted! Yet, the following week end could be a mad house of frenzied activity, with everyone running around, complaining about being absolutely exhausted, and praying for the door bell to stop ringing.

We did not always get along with fellow co-workers. We were, at times, subjected to outrageous requests and demands placed upon our minds, bodies and spirits.

And of course, we didn't like working long hours and spending extended periods of time away from our families and loved ones.

But all in all -- The money was usually good.

I guess this explains why in 1996 there were thousands of legal licensed prostitutes employed in the Silver State of Nevada, the last "Wild West" region of legal Brothels in the U.S.

CHAPTER EIGHT

Summary

We do not want to paint a picture of doom and gloom about the business of legalized prostitution in the State of Nevada, nor do we want to convey an image of sweetness and light.

We found that the most successful, emotionally and financially speaking, were those girls that were able to throw the switch, when they showed up at work. They could go from wife, mother, girlfriend, friend, daughter, or sister to working girl in zero to ten seconds, simply with a toss of their hair, a wig, or a line of blood red color placed on their lips.

After Brotheldom

As the years go on, some of us do get tired. We do grow older. Our dreams and goals change. We may even want to get married and live happily ever after in our little cottages with white picket fences. Or we might want to work for ourselves, as we grow tired of giving up half of the money we make to the owners of the Brothels.

It could be that we become greedy and want it all for ourselves. We also become disillusioned with the world, because of our warped perspective of always being "locked up". We get tired of our bodies being used over and over again. We get numb and desensitized to any emotional or physical feelings if we stay inside Brotheldom too long.

Like good little addicts that we are -- we keep coming back for more -- because we see no way out. We tend to be very co-dependent women, obsessive, excessive, obedient, submissive -- part of the flock falling into the fold -- caught up inside our own repeated patterns of behavior. Only occasionally can someone ever break loose of the tight reigns those patterns hold -- as in any classic addictive behavior (ask any alcohol or drug addict).

A Single Society

Our society seems so filled with single people because of the divorce rate, or by choice while pursuing or building careers. Many men we see at the ranches are tired of the bar scene as a place to "pick up" women. They're tired of "wining and dining" them and then, only, maybe getting laid.

They tell us that it's usually much cheaper just to come out to a ranch, and know for sure they're going to get what they want. It really does seem much more honest to not lie or deceive a woman into believing that maybe this man really does care about her or a possible relationship, when all he really wants is to "get laid"!

We get many men that are newly divorced or widowed and have not been out in the dating world for so many years that they don't know what to do. They're afraid of rejection, or they don't want to be in a relationship again, too soon, but they're missing the closeness that physical intimacy brings and so they come out to the ranches hoping to find those missing elements in their otherwise well-rounded lives.

I had one customer who had not even touched a woman for four years after his only wife had died. He came to the Brothel, I held him and he cried. He was so grateful just to have a woman touch him. It moved me too. I received a letter from him shortly after he left the ranch thanking me. He also wanted to marry me (as many customers do). I gently replied, "No thank you." I guess he had all the money he needed, but was rather lost and wandering now in his RV, traveling around, but feeling unfulfilled and lonely.

Many single men use our services. Some are extremely busy, successful executives who have not scheduled the time necessary for fulfilling their social life (physical and emotional needs). While others just don't want to get involved in a relationship. They prefer to use our services for any intimate physical contact or closeness with a woman, so they can just walk away when finished with fulfilling their needs, without any time-consuming commitments or entangled involvement.

There is also something "very real" happening in these houses or ranches inside Brotheldom out in the sticks in Nevada.

Sisters of the Heart

Maybe, it's because we can be "real" here -- open and honest. We can talk straight, nobody needs to "pull any punches," or "play any games," or cover anything up to hide their wants and desires. We just let it all hang out -- customers, girls, and management alike.

The customers do seem to be very grateful that they don't have to sneak around, feeling guilty because they are doing something illegal. We can all be whomever and whatever we want here and nobody seems to care (providing we stay within a few minor rules and guidelines outlined by the state, county, and each individual brothel).

I have found kindness and gentleness, softness and tenderness in these Brothels that I have rarely experienced in the outside world (by choices I have made in my encounters). I have experienced some of my deepest moments of emotion, here in this institutionalized world, such passive tenderness and non-aggressiveness, that has touched me deeply, "in my core," and will last me a lifetime.

Burn Out

At the same time, I have gotten so far out of touch with reality, that my make-believe world inside the Brothel has become my only reality. I have been carrying that lifestyle over into the other real world, outside the Brothel. I have definitely been working here too long.

I have encased myself in my own self-imposed little glass bubble -- shell. I have allowed strangers to be intimate physically with me over and over again. So much so, that when I'm now in the outside world, I have mixed that up with strangers I meet there, even though I don't allow them to get physical with me (like inside the Brothel). I open up completely emotionally to these perfect strangers. I open up too much, too soon.

I am trying to make changes to bridge that gap and reinfiltrate myself back into the world of reality. I am slowly realizing that I have been trying to justify working in a Brothel to make myself feel okay about myself.

I have been redefining reality for myself to make my life style and work okay, so I don't appear to be a bad person to myself. Is it self-preservation, or justifying, redefining my limits and morals? I am reflecting and really digging down deep into my soul and questioning myself and my actions, and really trying to evaluate and reevaluate everything I am doing as I try to make my transition to the world outside of Brotheldom.

Being locked inside for 24 hours a day for half of one's life each year for the last few years has cut down on the time when I would normally be outside mingling with people. I am starting to see how screwed up emotionally I am starting to get -- so needy of individual, intimate attention from males or females, friends or anybody that cares about me.

So, if I don't have enough intimate friends, I watch myself start to dress provocatively, on the street, to get attention -- any kind of attention, good or bad, from total strangers. Remember, I'm not as aggressive here on the outside and not as sure of myself. So, if you see someone on the street really dressed "hot", looking lost and lonely, maybe take time for a smile or a friendly hello -- it could be me ....

PROLOGUE

This book has been written to present facts. It has not been written to glorify the Brothel lifestyle or the profession of Prostitution or the customers that visit these establishments and should in no way be misconstrued to encourage woman to join the ranks of working girls or men to frequent these houses. We all have the right to make our own choices in our lives.

As a former Brothel participant I can relate to you some of my discoveries about myself in this prologue.

I had a wonderful joyous time my first two years in this business. I gave each customer my full heart for that time I was with them. I loved each and every one of them. I had fun playing dress up and felt light hearted happy and free and couldn't understand why the girls who had been in this business longer were so negative and depressed all the time.

Then after two years, it started to hit me too. I found myself being an actress more and more and not coming from the heart. Money became foremost and important. The fun was gone.

I tried to quit the business two years ago, but only lasted six months. My health was so run down that I had no choice but to quit. I was physically exhausted, a basket case.

Then, when I regained my physical health, I did not want to return to the Brothels, but knowing no other alternative where I could make the most amount of money for the least amount of time, and being addicted to it's powerful draw of money, sex and intensity, I went back for another six month tour of duty.

This time I only worked one week at a time, trying to maintain my sanity with two weeks off in between, but my heart was completely out of my work, and I could only see the money. It truly became an act with no heart behind the smile.

My physical and emotional health and sanity were at a bottom again last Spring and I left the Brothels once again, vowing to never come back. It was truly over this time.

I have only seen two customers, these past nine months, once I serviced a man, and one weekend I had sex when I didn't want to under the guise of a relationship.

Like any good addict, I am now pouring all my energy into creative endeavors, but trying very hard to balance my life with walking, talking, singing, laughing, dancing, sharing, spending time alone, and time with people. I feel like a new baby being born -- making new friends and learning to socialize outside of Brotheldom.

I am an addict. I have never used drugs or alcohol, but I am an addict in every other area of my life. I can be obsessive over sex, cuz it feels good, over food, over work, over play, over men, over women, over exercising, over creative works, over intensities and highs, you name it I can obsess over it. Every minute of every day I live with controlling my behavior. I want to integrate all my new patterns of existence together with a new joy and spirituality.

I used to set myself up in the past -- so that I had no alternative but return to the Brothel, because that was a guaranteed roof over my head, food and a weekly paycheck. I recognized the set-up now, but have to really struggle to find non-Brothel alternatives. I do not want to go back to the Brothels. I have lots of education, several college degrees and I enjoy drawing and writing.

Sometimes, as I reflect back, I think maybe I was rebelling against my puritanical upbringing and the puritanical consciousness imbedded into our society and culture and our hearts and minds. Maybe I went to an extreme to get over my deeply engrained notions that sex was bad and dirty, and certain sexual acts were naughty.

I realized that each time I had entered an Adult bookstore a few times in my past, I felt this cloud of shame over my head, like I was doing something I shouldn't be doing. But the last time I entered an Adult Bookstore, doing research for this project, it was OK. It was just another store -- that cloud had left. Maybe my Puritanical cloud has left my life now -- after four years of working in Brothels and nine months of therapy. I'm sure there must be other ways.

I hope that by you reading this book may be an easier way. I hope that we can all overcome our societal myths and stigmas that we have placed on all working girls, that they are bad, dirty, naughty girls that can't get a decent job.

I hope we can now look at Brothels and all working girls and customers as human beings, just like you and me brought into those situations by circumstance, unresolved family situations, codependencies, addictions, education, and by choice, etc. It is our choice to live our lives each day however we want. My choice of job is no better or worse than your choice. My reasons for choosing the job are no better or worse than your reasons. We each change and grow and learn everyday.

I hope that judgement and prejudice are a thing of the past decades -- that we no longer need to put other people down to make ourselves OK -- that we each have enough self-confidence and self-love to accept others lifestyles and choices. We may not agree with other people's actions, jobs or lifestyles but we can accept and allow -- isn't that the original democratic American ideal -- as long as we aren't harming other people?

BROTHEL GLOSSARY

1. **AIDS -** acquired immune deficiency syndrome

2. **BISEXUAL -** sex with men and women

3. **BOUDOIR -** bedroom

4. **BROTHEL -** House of Prostitution, Houses, Ranches, Cat House, Whorehouse, Bordello

5. **BROTHELDOM -** all aspects pertaining to the Brothel Industry

6. **CLIMAX -** getting off, cumming

7. **CONDOMS -** rubbers, raincoats

8. **DENTAL DAMS -** protection device used while giving oral sex. to a woman

9. **DOGGIE STYLE -** male penis penetration of a female vagina while both are down on all fours (or standing) from behind

10. **DOMINANCE** - one person ordering another person to perform sexual activities

11. **EARLY UP** - a listing of girls who have booked the least amount of money for the day in the brothel who are required to get up when door bells ring in the middle of the night

12. **ERECTION** - hard raised penis, stiff dick

13. **FANTASIES** - different ways of stimulating or achieving sexual gratification one dreams about

14. **FOREPLAY** - sexually arousing activities prior to orgasm and/or ejaculation

15. **GREEK** - anal sex, sodomy

16. **HALF AND HALF** - begins with oral sex being performed by the female on the male completed by conventional intercourse

17. **HIV** - human immune deficiency virus, the virus that causes AIDS. A sexually transmitted disease

18. **HOSTESS** - shift manager who greets customers at a Brothel

19. **IMPLANTS** - objects inserted into the sexual organs for enhancement, enlargement

20. **LINE UP** - prostitutes standing in a row infront of a customer so they may choose a partner for paid sexual activities

21. **LUBRICANT** - thick gooey substance applied to penis (or condom) and/or vagina for smooth penetration, KY Jelly, Astroglide

22. **MADAME** - female owner and/or manager of a Brothel (sometimes former working girls)

23. **MASSAGE** - touching and/or manipulating skin with hands or devices

24. **MASTURBATION** - solo sex without a partner

25. **MISSIONARY** - man on top of a woman during intercourse

26. **NONOXYNOL 9** - additive to lubricant which kills HIV virus

27. **ORAL SEX** (for men) - blow job, face, head

28. **ORAL SEX** (for women) - going down, eating pussy, French

29. **ORGASM** (for woman) - climax, cum, getting off, vaginal orgasm, clitoral orgasm, G spot orgasm

30. **PASSING** - girls working in Brothels who have booked the most money during the day who are allowed to sleep at a certain time.

31. **PENILE IMPLANTS** - rods, tissue objects inserted surgically into the penis

32. **PIMP** - an individual living off the earnings of a prostitute

33. **PROSTITUTES** - working girls, ladies of the evening or night, hookers, hoes

34. **PROSTITUTION** - exchanging sexual services for money

35. **PUMPS** - small vacuum pumps which fill up a bag which has been surgically implanted in the penis

36. **RINGS** - metal rings inserted around the penis to keep the hard on longer

37. **SENSUOUS MASSAGE** - erotic use of hands on the body, stimulating the senses

38. **SEX** - intercourse, making love, fucking, screwing, getting laid

39. **SEXUALLY TRANSMITTED DISEASE (STD)** - STD's infect the sexual and reproductive organs and sometimes cause general body infections. STD's are spread during vaginal, anal and oral sex and by contact with infected blood. STD germs infect the mouth, rectum and sex organs (Gonorrhea, Chlyamydia, Herpes, Syphilis, AIDS)

40. **SIXTY NINE (69)** - oral sex between two people simultaneously

41. **SPECIALTY PARTIES** - types of activities offered by a prostitute - couples, handicaps, racial, Two Girl Shows, Titty Fuck, etc.

42. **TITTY FUCK** - penis is on a woman's chest between her breasts for sexual stimulation and/or cumming

43. **TWO GIRL PARTY** - Two girls cater to the sexual needs of one man simultaneously

44. **TWO GIRL SHOW** - Two girls make love with each other while a man and/or woman watch

45. **TURN OUT** (T.O.) - a girl who is working as a prostitute for the first time

46. **VIBRATOR** - electrically operated sexual device used for sexual stimulation

Look
For Other
BROTHEL BOOKS
Available
Soon

BROTHEL DIARIES

Personal diaries of girls while working in the Nevada Brothels. Details of customer parties, preferences, emotions, feelings and how we catered to their every wish and desire and made their fantasies come true while fulfilling our own special needs.

BROTHEL DIRECTORY

A complete "up-date" listing of Nevada Brothels -- north and south. Includes Addresses, phone numbers, directions, photos, location map and information.

Sisters of the Heart
P.O. Box 94534
Las Vegas, NV 89193